PRAISE FOR *NAILING IT*

'It's rare for comedians to be as funny on paper as they are on stage, but Rich Hall nails it. He is clearly a writer at heart, and his true tales about life on the stand-up comedy circuit are hilarious, touching and bravely personal'
Carl Hiaasen

'I loved this book. Absolutely adored it. I devoured it and savoured every word. A wild and wonderful love letter to comedy'
Adam Hills

'Rich Hall is a comedic maverick with a laser eye for detail. He is as funny as he is fearless. This book is no exception . . . a kaleidoscopic journey through the twists and turns of his comedy and his life'
Lewis Black

'So well written . . . Buy it right now and prepare to be amazed'
Merrill Markoe

'Since 1978, Rich Hall has made me laugh with a most original and creative brand of stand-up comedy. Now the bastard has written the best comedy memoir I've ever read. I've about had it with this guy'
Ritch Shydner

'Hall is good company . . . writing with wise-cracking, conversational ease . . . Will have you chuckling throughout with its amusing collection of well-spun yarns'
Irish Times

Rich Hall is a multi award-winning American comedian, musician and author. In the US he wrote for David Letterman and appeared on David's show frequently as a guest. He was also a cast member and writer for *Saturday Night Live*, *Fridays* and *Not Necessarily The News*. In 1998, he created his alter-ego Otis Lee Crenshaw, a redneck jailbird from Tennessee, which won him a Perrier Award at Edinburgh in 2000. He moved to the UK in 2001, and has been touring the country and appearing on numerous British TV shows since, including *Have I Got News For You* and *QI* (he once held the record for the most 'wins'). Rich has also written and presented ten highly acclaimed documentaries for BBC Four. He lives with his wife, Karen, alternating between homes in West London and Livingston, Montana. *Nailing It* is his fourth book.

NAILING IT!

TALES FROM THE COMEDY FRONTIER

RICH HALL

QUERCUS

First published in Great Britain in 2022 by Quercus Editions Ltd
This paperback published in 2023 by

QUERCUS

Quercus Editions Ltd
Carmelite House
50 Victoria Embankment
London EC4Y 0DZ

An Hachette UK company

A CIP catalogue record for this book is available
from the British Library

PB ISBN 978 1 52942 245 0
Ebook ISBN 978 1 52942 246 7

10 9 8 7 6 5 4 3 2 1

Typeset by CC Book Production
Printed and bound in Great Britain by Clays Ltd, Elcograf S.p.A.

Papers used by Quercus are from well-managed forests and other responsible sources.

For Karen, Dixie and Hayes

'Fortunately, I keep my feathers numbered for just such an emergency.'

Foghorn Leghorn

CONTENTS

PREFACE

As a teenager, I would sit in a mountain pass of back issues of mystery magazines – *Alfred Hitchcock, Ellery Queen, Mike Shayne, Manhunt* – devouring every word. School was a waste of time, a con game. I was fourteen and felt entitled to a payout for what had already amounted to years of scholastic incarceration. I fancied myself a writer. I had one of those green-keyed Smith Coronas that sat on my cramped bedroom desk asserting an authority beyond my years. It hammered out each letter with a satisfying report like gunfire.

I would walk home from baseball practice thinking not of runs, hits and errors, but of plots and scenarios. I wrote furiously and sent off my stories, always with a self-addressed return envelope and a proper cover letter – which, I imagine, is as far as most editors got.

Dear Sirs:
Enclosed is a submission for your magazine which I consume
voraciously. Please be kind enough to read my manuscript as
I hope it meets your high standards of quality mystery writing.
    Richard Hall

Every afternoon I checked the mail on the kitchen table. Nothing. No acceptance letters, no checks, no returned manuscripts. This was a bigger mystery than anything I was cranking out. *Where the hell were my stories going?*

My dad ran a specialty foods operation – really, just a small warehouse unit at the edge of town. But he'd hired an answering service to create the impression of a bigger operation. Projection was everything to him, so he must have figured my *desire* to be an author outweighed any discernible talent.

On Christmas morning he presented me with a bound leather scrapbook. Inside was all the missing correspondence.

'Look there,' he said excitedly. He pointed to an *Alfred Hitchcock* memo carefully mounted onto the thick burnished page.

Dear Author:
Thank you for the opportunity to read your manuscript. Unfortunately, it does not meet our needs at this time. We wish you the best of luck in finding a publisher for your story elsewhere.
The Editors

I examined each scrapbook page with lingering, hot disappointment. 'Dad, these are all rejection letters.'

'Indeed, they are. But you'll notice they all designate you as an *author*. That's the encouraging thing.' This detail seemed entirely strategic to him. He believed he understood me, without ever actually listening to a word I said.

'All you have to do now,' he said, placing a hand on my shoulder for gravitas, 'is learn to write a *whole* lot better. Merry Christmas, son.'

Although I aspired to be a writer, I trained to be a journalist. But I ended up a comedian. Probably because cold, dry facts never interested me – *who, where, why, when* or *what*. I was more intrigued by *what if*? Verisimilitude.

Here, then, are some stories. They're not about glitz, or fame, or agents named Swifty or how I met my seventh wife at the rehab clinic and found spiritual direction. None of that shit happened to me. These are stories about the crux of the comedy moment – in both my professional and personal life – where I had to *nail it*. Screwball turn-of-events, wayward characters, unplanned disasters and *something-wonderful-right-away* moments that made my life funny by happenstance, while I was busy trying to manufacture it. They're not all triumphs, but if someone propped me up at the end of the comedy bar and put a quarter in me, these are the tunes I would spin.

Rich Hall, 2022

CHAPTER 1

MISFIT

With their wholesome faces and the kind of square, gleaming teeth that can only be produced by a region abundant in corn, grain and cereal, students cross the commons of a state university in Manhattan, Kansas, on an unseasonably warm October afternoon in 1977. They are drawn to a curious sight: a wooden stool on which sits a clear jug of water, a large easel supporting a shrouded painting, a carton of dog treats and a plastic bucket marked *Tithings*.

What have we here?

In the middle of this tableau stands a young man with a loudhailer. He wears a cheap white linen suit. His nervousness isn't visible, but it's there, deep in his gut – steady and expanding. He switches the device on to speak. This is the moment: call me Reverend Milkbone.

'Where will your dog spendeth eternity!' I shout. 'Bring them forth so that they shall be saved! "For they are shepherds who have no understanding", Isaiah 56:11.'

The small crowd looks around. There are no dogs in evidence.

'Sally forth ye and deliver me a mutt, a mongrel, a pure-breed. The Lord does not judge the dog by its lineage. Only the American Kennel Club does that. I will baptize any dog within a quarter-mile radius!'

'Why?' someone yells.

'Why what, brother?'

'Why are you baptizing dogs?'

'If not me, then who? "For all God's creatures great and small shall go to heaven", Ecclesiastes: something-or-another. But first they must be absolved of sin. Read your Bible son.'

More students are gathering now. A frisson of amusement permeates the air – a shared sense of an inside joke. I stride over to the mysterious covered painting. Both the sturdy easel on which it perches and the striped drop cloth that obscures it were purchased from an art supply superstore on the outskirts of Joplin, Missouri.

'You have seen da Vinci's *The Last Supper*, have you not?' I call through the loudhailer, unaware that the high, thin frequencies of the device probably *are* being picked up by several dogs in the vicinity. 'We all know of course that *The Last Supper* depicts the Eucharist before Christ's crucifixion! Well, brothers and sisters, there is a similar event in canine theology!'

Where is this going, the crowd wonders.

With a deft showman's flair, I whip the drop cloth away to reveal a large portrait of Dogs Playing Poker. Laughter of recognition from the crowd. An encouraging sign.

'Behold the atmosphere of impending betrayal. The Doberman Pinscher – clearly a stand-in for our Lord Jesus Christ – dominates

4

the painting. All eyes are upon him. But note the bulldog – Judas! – slipping the ace of clubs under the table to his co-conspirator. And yet, the Doberman chooses to forgive them. He's been dealt a lousy hand – a pair of nines – and proclaims unto his brethren, "Know that I shall be raised!"'

More laughter.

I am conscious of the surge of adrenalin within – what they call the *performance rush*. How far can I take this? It's a barrage of possibilities. I have rehearsed this routine a hundred times. From behind the steering wheel of my truck driving across endless prairie roads. In diner parking lots. In empty cornfields, blathering quite insanely at crows. Holed up at night in off-ramp motel rooms, feverishly making notes onto legal pads, mouthing words and choreographing gestures in front of a full-length mirror to get the cadences and rhythms just right. This is the trial run. If it all falls flat, I will hastily gather my props, hightail it to my truck, peel out of Manhattan, Kansas, and never look back.

More onlookers straggle forth. The crowd begins to swell in volume and excitement. Then, from the back of the gathering, the sound of raucous barking.

'Bring that dog forward,' I call. 'Hasten to Reverend Milkbone!'

The dog is led to the front of the crowd. Its owner is a wide-faced kid with careless shoulder-length hair and a Frisbee. Probably a freshman up for any hijinks. The dog is an Irish Setter of vacant charm. I take the kid's Frisbee, wave it under the dog's nose and shoot it out over the crowd. It lands atop the portico of the administration building. The dog takes off, loses his sense of purpose and trots back.

'"For what gaineth a dog if its soul goes up on the roof and he can't get it down".' To the owner: 'What is this dog's name?'

'Bandit. That was my Frisbee, man . . .'

'Bandeth?'

'*Bandit.*'

'That's what I said. Reverend Milkbone has a lithp. What is your name?'

'Todd.'

'Do you know your Old Testament, Todd? Numbers 1 and 6?'

'No.'

'Well, you should. It's your football team's win-loss record.'

Whoops of recognition.

'Does Bandeth accept that Jesus Christ is God's only solution for sin and for salvation?'

'I dunno.'

'Does Bandeth understandeth he is helpless to earn God's favor simply by being a *good boy*?'

'I dunno.'

'Does he wish to partake of the sacrament?'

'The what?'

'THE SACRAMENT!' I scream at the guy through the loudhailer, although it is literally only inches from his face. 'WILL THE DOG BREAK BREAD WITH ME?'

'Yes!' the kid shouts back, realizing he needs to play along.

I reach into the treat box and remove a dog biscuit, mealy-red and shaped like a cartoon bone. I snap it in two and proffer one half to Bandit, who willfully gulps it down. Then, for just a moment, I drop character and speak offhandedly. 'This is not only a holy sacrament, people. It actually says on the box "for whiter teeth". To be honest, I don't think a dog cares if its teeth are white or not. It's drinking out of the toilet for Chrissakes . . . sorry, Lord. If I was a dog, I'd be a lot more concerned about that black rubbery stuff forming around my mouth. What in God's name is that? A *gasket*?'

Big laughter. I'm feeling a kind of emancipation of spirit now, of total control, of holding these strangers in thrall. I bring the other half of the biscuit up to my mouth slowly, feigning dread – a showy carnival barker's build-up. The crowd signals its encouragement.

'Eat it!' they chant.

I shrug and pop it into my mouth, chew it experimentally, take an exaggerated pause and convulse in disgust, gagging, grasping at my throat, making sounds like a seagull. I stagger into the crowd, grab several shoulders for mock support, stagger back again, drop to my knees, pound my own shoulder blades and cough the offending object out onto the ground.

The crowd greets this pantomime with furious delight. Good old-fashioned, gross-out comedy.

'That is the most disgusting thing I've ever tasted in my life,' I croak, then grab another one from the box. 'Hmm, maybe I just got a bad one.' I chew this one up and swallow it nonchalantly. Applause. The tipping point, that part. I am aware of the surge of confidence from the crowd, faith in the form of laughter. Then Bandit is summoned to the water pitcher. I instruct his owner to hold him still.

'Bandeth, do you believe in the redemption of flea dip? The sanctity of the fire hydrant? The final squirrel? Do you believe that pretending to be something we're not is our only crack at release from the bondage of accountability? That God is up there, He's ours and He plays a mean Telecaster?' Bandit's tail whips from side to side like a metronome. 'I'll take that as a yes. In obedience to our Lord and Savior, Jesus Christ, and upon your profession of faith, I baptize you, big fella, in the name of the Father, Son and Holy Spirit. Amen.'

I pour out the water and it streams down the dog's banjo-shaped skull.

'Reject Satan with all your might!'

The dog, of course, shakes himself spasmodically. The crowd goes nuts. It occurs to me it's not always going to go this swimmingly and, sooner or later, I'm going to get bitten.

Later, when the gig is over, I slump in my truck seat, feeling what might be described as an agony of relief, like I've pulled off some extravagant heist. There is an urgency to process what just transpired, to edit, to improve. Nothing in my past has ever felt this vital, and all questions of ambition, or lack thereof, are now null and void.

I dump the contents of the plastic bucket onto the seat beside me and sort through it. Sixteen dollars and forty-five cents – mostly in coins – two joints, a tab of acid and a St Christopher medal. I open the glove compartment, unfold a map and study it. Kansas University at Lawrence is to the east. Wichita State University to the south. I calculate the sky and see it is clear to the south. Wichita it is. I start up the truck motor. I am reinvented: a comedian.

Let's have it now: what led to this? Any number of things from that epoch could be said to have pushed me toward a life of comedy. A certain young woman, for example. Or the self-understanding that I was not remotely what you would call a *responsible* adult.

Earlier in July of that year, I'd hugged my folks goodbye in the driveway of our house on Brandywine Avenue in Charlotte, North Carolina. I was twenty-three, just graduated from college and had been offered a desk position at the *Knoxville News Sentinel* in Tennessee. Like Tom Joad, I climbed into my old Chevy Apache, loaded down with my belongings, and coaxed the engine to life. The paint-can rattle of the truck's worn pistons hardly raised an eyebrow on this shabby street, accustomed as it was to the ceaseless artillery of flatulent tailpipes and peeling tires. I pulled away. My parents waved.

I supposed big things were expected of me. The idea of having an actual *desk* seemed to hold special wonderment for my dad. His parting advice was, 'Keep your head down for the first month of the job and get the read on things before you make your move.' How can I be a journalist with my head down? I intended to take the blue highways across the entire expanse of the trip, a rehearsal for what I considered my current position in life: to take notice of *everything*.

What I failed to notice, not twenty minutes later, was the wing mirror on a Cadillac Eldorado parked in the circular driveway of John T. Sullivan's home in the swanky Foxcroft section of Charlotte. That the car was parked carelessly is debatable. I clipped it with my own wing mirror and sheared it right off, brackets and all.

Typical. It seemed I could never visit my girlfriend, Erin Sullivan, at her parents' home without an exquisitely uncomfortable encounter of some kind. I'd driven over to say goodbye. She was going off to grad school in Missouri. I was bound for Tennessee. We'd been together for a year and a half. This necessary crisis had been slowly building, but, because we'd never talked about it, I wasn't sure how our future was going to play out.

I picked the mirror up from the driveway and noted my fragmented reflection in about six or eight pieces of broken glass, so there's your requisite but admittedly flimsy foreshadowing. I carried the mangled thing to the front door. The brass knocker on the recessed entrance read, 'SULLIVAN' in wrought, majuscule lettering. Beneath this, a bewildering Celtic crest proclaimed dubious animal ancestry: an elk to be exact – half black, half white. There are not, nor have there ever been, elk in Ireland.

I lifted the knocker and the door opened on the upstroke. Mattie, the Sullivan's black maid stood there, dressed in a yellow apron with white flounce trim, her broad face beaming: the total plantation get-up.

'Hello, Mattie.'

'Hello, Mr Hall. You come to say goodbye to Erin? I expect she's out back at the pool.'

'I need to see Mr Sullivan first.'

'What have you got there?'

'A little accident.'

'Oh my, my. Come on in.'

I followed Mattie into the dining room where John T. and the Missus were seated at opposite ends of a long mahogany table, dining in glaring silence. Mrs Sullivan, striking in a country-club kind of way, acknowledged my presence with a patrician and artificial smile. Her hair was done up in a tight athletic twist. A pair of oxblood-colored driving gloves and a matching purse sat on the edge of the table. John T. didn't bother to disguise his inhospitality. He dropped a spoon emphatically into his bowl of chowder to endorse my unwelcome existence in his daughter's life. His thick fingers, raw and red-knuckled, ended in perfectly clipped nails. Real rags-to-riches hands.

'What have you brought into my house?'

'I'm afraid I clipped the mirror on the car outside.'

He stood up and made a big deal of being inconvenienced.

'Mattie!' he called out. Mattie, who had disappeared, reappeared. 'Mattie. Find Ruiz and ask him to sweep up the mess in the driveway, will you?' He took the wing mirror from me without bothering to examine it and set it down on a sideboard cabinet. 'I'll call my insurance agent in the morning. You'll need to leave your details.' He returned to his seat, plucked the soup spoon from the bowl and shot his wrist out with a little flourish, as if he were about to sign a big, fat document.

'Oh, I don't think that's necessary, Mr Sullivan. It's just a scrape. You can send me the repair bill. I'm good for it.'

He spooned some chowder into his mouth – lobster no doubt, probably flown in fresh from New England – chewing predatorily as he talked with marvelous accuracy. 'If I bill you, I get a new mirror. If I bill your insurance company, I get a whole new door. *(Chomp)* New sill plates. New threshold plates. High-level, custom trim package. One set of billet locks. *(Chomp)* I'm a property developer, son. It's all second nature to me.' He swallowed and narrowed his grey eyes. 'Tell me you're not driving around in that decrepit truck of yours uninsured . . .'

'I sort of let it lapse,' I said weakly.

John T. made a fist around his soup spoon in a way that weaponized it. I could tell he was gathering up some real red-meat words. To be fair, I had it coming, and I braced myself.

Blessedly, Erin appeared in the dining-room doorway. She was wearing a white cotton robe, toweling her long wild black curls vigorously in that way that some women do, where they tilt their head and lean – really lean – into it.

Ask me: Was she a looker? Yes, in an unconventional way. She was tall and studious-looking with an arresting gaze. Irish handsome, you might say – but Southern-fried. She was self-owned and cheerfully alert, and she had an unironic enthusiasm for all the things her upbringing offered: stylishness, books, comportment, travel. What she saw in me, I was never quite sure. We made each other laugh, I know that much. She tended to stare at me a lot, deep and assessing, almost as if I were an exhibit. Then a grin would break out on her face, a big old Southern grin that made you think of pecan pie and drum majorettes. That was the thing I wanted to isolate – that gentility.

Among other things.

'Hello,' she said in a sandpapery voice. She was never completely comfortable with me in her parent's house – too much friction.

'Hi,' I said back. 'Your dad was just about to round up on me.'

John T. simmered. 'I was merely about to explain to young Richard here the folly of driving without insurance.' He lowered on me. 'For starters, it's a Cook's tour of our vaunted county correctional facility.'

Me: 'As is claims fraud . . .'

Mrs Sullivan: 'Is it even possible to enjoy a civil lunch at this table?'

Erin: 'Why don't you fellas settle this with a good, old-fashioned *arm-wrassle!*'

John T.: 'But more to the point, it shows your utter lack of respect for innocent lives. What if Mrs Sullivan here had been stepping out of that car when you came tearing through? You have no provision for *personal injury.*'

Mrs Sullivan: 'John, dear, try to think of me as more than one of your actuarial figures.'

Me: 'In all fairness, Mr Sullivan, if your wife were stepping out of a car, *no* one would hit her.' I turned and gave Mrs Sullivan my most winsome smile. 'She has the kind of looks that would stop traffic.'

Boom. I laid that down like a gambler fanning a royal flush across a poker table. Mrs Sullivan made a small *o* with her mouth and trailed her eyes across the length of the dining room. Erin buried her face in her towel stifling a laugh. John T. Sullivan rose from the table in full bluster.

'No one talks to my wife like that!' he bellowed.

'Oh, of course they do,' said Erin.

A look of indignation as can only be produced by an inconvenienced Southern patriarch in his own goddamn dining room shot from Erin to the missus to me. I was ready for a showdown – if I thought Erin was on my side. But it was part of her style to play both sides, like a double agent. She looked at me and made the smallest nod with her head: *outside.*

Later, the two of us were sitting by the edge of the pool, Erin making lazy eights in the water with her long, tanned legs.

'Remove your hand from my thigh,' she said.

'Right.'

'Curtains are twitching . . .'

'Right.'

'And you can stop looking so pleased with yourself. "Looks that could stop traffic." Jeez. You should be a comedian.' Spoken as a throwaway aside.

'Actually, I meant it in a wildlife sense. Like an elk in the middle of the road.'

'That's harsh.'

'I don't care. Your mom despises me.'

'Correction: Dad despises you. My mother just thinks . . .'

'Thinks what?'

'Well, she says you're a scratch at the starting gate.'

'Ahhhhh.' I let that sink in.

She pulled a pack of Salems from her robe pocket and lit one. I watched her with dumb fascination. Erin smoked like she was being filmed in a cinema close-up: thumb anchored to jawline, swiveling it downward between extended fingers to meet her lips. Her eyes – silvery and drawn at the corners – half-closed as she inhaled. No one smoked a cigarette more vividly.

Finally, I said, 'Wanna discuss the future?'

'Unpredictable.'

'Review the past?'

'Unreliable.'

Silence.

'I should hit the road then.'

'Buy some goddamn insurance.'

More silence.

I said, 'Once I'm settled in Knoxville, I'll come see you. Yes . . . no?'

She adopted a hillbilly twang. 'It's a mighty fur piece from Tennessee to Missouri.'

'Five hundred and six miles to be exact. Drive it in no time.'

'Well, then, suit yourself. I'll have my head in the books most of the time.'

'I'll just have to nail you from behind.'

'Ok!' she said chirpily. 'And I'll pretend it's someone else.'

'Good one.' After a moment: '"Scratch at the starting gate"?'

'Uh-huh.'

'She said that?'

'Mm-hmm.'

'Tell me, what do *you* think?'

She took a drag, exhaled and diffused the smoke around her with a wave of the hand, a film noir effect. 'I'm inclined to agree.'

I pulled out of the Sullivan's driveway and headed west, thinking, *did we just break up?*

I didn't turn on the radio for two hours, until I'd reached the foothills of the Smoky Mountains – just watched the yellow center line ticking in front of me. Every small town was awash in flags and tricolor bunting. The nation was celebrating its birthday, and I tried to convince myself I was celebrating my own freedom! Free to take any road, sleep at any motel, eat Old South barbeque! (Putting exclamation points at the end of my thoughts made everything more upbeat!) Erin and I were broken up. Somewhere right before the Black Mountain turnoff, I came to grips with this reality and accepted it with concise unemotional logic. Neither of us really knew what we wanted, so it was best to break up because, like I said, neither of us knew what we wanted, which, when you think about it, is a very special thing for two people to have in common, therefore, we definitely belonged together.

I turned off at Black Mountain.

I drove to a town called Cullowhee and cruised through the campus of my alma mater, Western Carolina University. I took an honor lap around the student newspaper building. I'd spent a good chunk of my four-year education there, editing the paper, drinking too much beer, surrounded by a staff of pedants and social outcasts. We swanned around in an atmosphere of self-importance, constantly looking for ways to ridicule the lousy football team, wage print vendettas against the administration and – in the conveniently reductive parlance of the seventies – *stick it to the man*. Oh yeah.

I parked the truck and walked down to the student union quad where I'd first met Erin, spring of my junior year. She'd been sitting on a wall reading *The Floating Opera* by John Barth, holding the book close to her face, like the two of them were having some kind of an argument. She sensed me staring at her, dropped it slightly, and spoke from behind the pages.

'I know who you are, newsboy.'

'And who are you?'

'Erin Sullivan.'

'What's *The Floating Opera* about, Erin Sullivan?'

She dropped the book to her lap, slightly harried. 'Oh . . . god . . . hard to even begin . . . so many layers.'

'Never mind. I'm going to read it myself. Then . . .'

'Then what?'

'Uhm . . . an exchange of amiable discourse!' This came out so cheerfully and grandiloquently stupid, it actually made her laugh.

'You're something of a clod, aren't you?' she said.

'Not usually.'

I bought a copy of the book and read it in one day. Well, *accreted* the words and the images to mind anyway. Editing a student newspaper had killed my ability to plumb layers. I only saw angles.

'Finished it,' I announced the next time I saw her.

'*Already*?'

'I'm a quick reader.'

'It's not a book to be wolfed down. Remind me never to go to dinner with you.'

'Want to go to dinner with me?'

You get the picture.

Back on the road. West of Cashiers, I bought a bag of roadside cherries and got stuck behind a lumber truck with chrome mudflaps in the shape of a voluptuous reclining woman. I spat the pits out the open window and wondered what it would be like to have a girlfriend so refreshingly one-dimensional.

Such thoughts were quickly doused by the God-fearing temperance of mountain country. A black, creosoted barn collapsed on one side, its roof exhorting 'Get Right With God' in violent white letters.

Outside Highlands, a rusty, battered Oldsmobile heaved sedately. The bumper sticker asked, 'Where will *you* spend eternity?' I had to consider that for a good twenty miles. A hog-auction-voiced preacher on the radio declared, 'God doesn't want hit-by-pitches, God wants home-runs.' It wasn't until I crossed into Tennessee that I felt I had put a line between God's play-calling and my slothful, slothful ways.

There were things in Tennessee that were just downright unsettling. Gatlinburg was a souvenir hellhole that appeared to view the indigenous Cherokee as prop comics: cheap rubber tomahawks, beadwork moccasins, garish war bonnets. A sign in front of a prefabricated teepee read, 'Reasonable prices. We won't scalp you.' Out of burlesque curiosity, I stopped to tour the Salt and Pepper Shaker Museum in Pigeon Forge. One room was devoted entirely to congenially racist memorabilia: ceramic blackamoors and mammies ranging in size from thimbles to industrial grinders.

I passed through a succession of hamlets that sounded like afflictions: Wartburg, Spurgeon and Soddy-Daisy. Then, through ones that sounded like their remedies: Tusculum, Jellico and New Hope.

Descending into Knoxville, my spirits rose with the lowering elevation. The outlying neighborhoods were humble, full of tight, wooden houses shaded by magnolia trees, gratuitous in their stateliness. Brusque-looking brick buildings with ghost murals advertised products that no longer existed: NuGrape Soda and Philco TVs. The whole town had a drowsy, bygone feel to it, like an old country song playing on a kitchen table radio. I absorbed this without bias. This was now, after all, my *beat*. I needed to get to know it inside out – and as quickly as possible, to prove myself a journalist.

That's been my whole life, basically: *proving.* Impressing upon coaches, teachers, peers, girlfriends that I am capable. But I'm not, really. I'm a competent imitation of capable. I suspected Erin knew that. I suspected she desired something more substantial in the way of a suitor. If she was out of my life – as I feared she might be – I was at a distinct loss of mission and that just wouldn't do.

I need to nail this, I told myself.

Turned out, all I needed to know about Knoxville was: who kicked the bucket.

My assignment at the *News Sentinel* was writing 'slot notices' – journalese for obituaries. The day crew would gather titbits on the decedent – cause of death, who survived them, etc. – jot it down on whatever was at hand, then toss it onto my desk. I would pick up a matchbook cover that read, 'Tazwell Edward 76', pair it with a cocktail napkin that read, 'Tazwell peacefully', and match that to the back of an envelope that read, 'Tazwell half-sister Maureen Tuscaloosa Alabama'. I was like the Magpie of Death. At night, when the place was dark and nearly empty, I had to assimilate these cryptic, necrotic noodlings into fitting words that committed souls I'd never met to everlasting peace.

My dreams began to fill up with dead people, so I took to staying up all night after work. There wasn't much to do at two a.m. in Knoxville. I didn't want to drink – coffee sufficed as much as anything. Once I drifted into an all-night bar called The Atlas, feeling like I needed to be more social. I tried to strike up a conversation with a *News Sentinel* copyeditor whose remit included writing the

'Daily Chuckle' and the 'Daily Prayer'. I figured he must have a morbid sense of humor.

'Why do people always die after a "long courageous battle with cancer"?' I asked him. 'Why do you never read "died kicking and screaming into the afterlife following repeated attempts at satanic pacts and various ritual goat sacrifices in their own basement"?'

He stared at me the way you'd stare at something that's been sitting at the back of the fridge for too long. Finally, he said, 'This used to be an accommodating atmosphere. I'm gonna find another place to do my drinking.'

I nursed my coffee and eavesdropped on the unfussy young barmaid chattering to someone at the end of the bar.

'Momma wants to go to Nashville, Daddy wants to go to Memphis, so they just stay home and fight. Lord, all I want is to go dancing.' I genuinely couldn't tell whether that was her lament or she was reciting the lyrics to a country song.

The following afternoon I knocked on my editor's cubicle. His name was either Banks Whitaker or Whitaker Banks. In an Old South town like Knoxville, you never quite knew which name came first.

'I'd like to try my hand at some feature stories,' I said.

'Knock yourself out. I'll look at them. But not at the expense of backlogged stiffs. That's your job.' He had one of those faces where the eye movements don't quite sync up with the mouth. It's possible he was shellshocked from the constant thrum of the linotype room above his desk.

'How long do I have to keep writing death notices?'

'Until people stop dying.' He laced his fingers behind his head, a completely inauthentic gesture. 'Remember this. You are the only writer here whose words have permanence. They will be laminated, placed inside Bibles and keepsake boxes. You chronicle the rhythm of someone's life and the sadness of their passing. If it means nothing to you, it means everything to the families. Think about that.'

'I'll try to keep that in mind.' I wondered how many times he'd given this pep talk.

'Anyway, we've got a computer program coming in to replace you. Then I'll bump you up to feature obits.'

'Is that normal hours?'

'Lemme guess, writing up the dead is giving you the fantods.'

'I'm having a little trouble sleeping.'

'You tried taking walks at night?'

'Yep.'

'Not helping?'

'I just feel like I'm passing the houses of the future dead.'

'There's no such thing as normal in the newspaper business, son. I sleep three, four hours tops. You wanna walk, get out to Oakwood or Farragut (he pronounced it *Fair-gut*). That's the affluent areas. You walk around this part of town too long, you'll be writing your own obituary.'

I took Whitaker's advice and, one night, walked all the way out to Farragut. Here the lawns were landscaped, and the only industrial hum came from swimming pool filters. You could smell the magnolias and balsams and new-cut grass. Most of Knoxville seemed to be hastening in a straight line to the end with no hope of renewal.

But here, luxury had a kind of eternal breadth to it. The word that came to mind was *Sullivan-esque*.

I lay down on one of the lawns, closed my eyes and saw Erin's face etched in a retinal image on my eyelids. I listened to the grass ticking and fell asleep.

I wrote up spec stories, but nothing came of them. A lawyer attempted to sue a rooster for violating noise abatement ordinances in west Knoxville. Hundreds of human teeth were discovered in a wall in Marysville when construction workers renovated the office of a retired dentist. Residents of Alcoa were finding dead sardines in their mailboxes. 'It's making my mail stink,' a baffled homeowner claimed. Local color. Everyday real-life stories. Filed under 'dead or non-pending'. This was my career: the dead were alive, and the alive were dead.

The automated obituary program never materialized, and I stayed mired in the same routine. I tried to make friends with other staff members, but the grim nature of my job kept them at a distance. I cracked jokes. They seemed to think I was coffin-measuring them. I felt like I was losing all fluency, that journalism was a dead-end career (!) and that I'd wasted an education. I wrote to the bursar of Western Carolina University and asked for all my money back.

Mostly though, I wrote letters to Erin. I'd always told her everything, true and false. She'd always showed a preference for the false. I told her I was making quite a name for myself as a maestro of the precious craft of *chronicling*. That I had interviewed the Cyclotron Women of the Oak Ridge Facility, the ones who monitored uranium isotopes in 1942, unaware they were helping build the atomic bomb. That I had consummated the memoirs of the world's oldest Confederate War survivor, now confined to an old folks' home in Smyrna. That I had witnessed the birth of a white buffalo, sacred in many cultures, on a farm outside LaFollette. Lies. Lies. Lies. That I had adopted a fedora and a rakish blue cravat. That I was short-listed for a Pulitzer. That I was missing her. That part was true. Stupid-crazy missing her. That I had a picture in my head of the two of us that was pure, page-one Americana raunch: she dressed in the flowing green garb of Lady Liberty, me as Uncle Sam, wielding carnal dynamite. Because I didn't have her address, I directed these fabulisms to 'Whom It May Concern: Dept. of Comparative Literature, Lindenwood College, St Charles, Missouri' with a request they be forwarded. Later – long after it had ceased to matter – I would learn they were opened by an associate dean of graduate studies named E.J. Thrift, who had acquired the serious hots for Erin. He read them with gleeful condescension and tossed them into a waste bin.

My apartment was near the University of Tennessee campus, so I spent a lot of time on the second floor of the Hodges library, reading, researching, composing my useless stories. I wasn't that long removed from the collegiate life, and I think I felt a little homesick. One late September afternoon, when the great square windows were thrown open to usher in the breeze, I heard a vaguely familiar voice curling up from the plaza.

'GOD DOESN'T WANT HIT-BY-PITCHES, GOD WANTS HOME-RUNS!'

I went to the window. A spirited crowd had gathered near the Europa statue, and they were jostling to get a view of the speaker.

'LET ME TELL YOU, BROTHERS AND SISTERS, SIN IS A CURVE BALL YOU CAN'T STEP BACK FROM.'

The man clutched a Bible in one hand, a loudhailer in the other. He wore a white linen suit and looked like a low-rent version of Robert Mitchum. This was real Southern Gothic, tent-revival stuff, jarringly out of place in such academic surroundings. By the time I got downstairs and joined the crowd, he'd transgressed from baseball metaphors to something far more caustic.

'GOD, CAN YOU TELL ME, 'CAUSE NO ONE DOWN HERE CAN,' he implored skyward, 'WHY ARE THERE WHOREHOUSES IN THIS TOWN WHEN ALL THESE CO-ED GIRLS ARE GIVING IT AWAY FOR FREE?'

This elicited a flurry of catcalls.

'They're spreading love, just like Jesus!' someone yelled.

'Troglodyte!' cried a female voice.

Someone else: 'Tell us more about these whorehouses!'

'Who is this guy?' I asked a student. She told me he was Jed Smock, itinerant campus evangelist.

'He comes through here two or three times a year,' she said. 'Stick around. It gets pretty heavy.'

Students were streaming in from every direction, drawn by the spectacle.

'WHEN IS THE LAST TIME ONE OF YOU GIRLS BLUSHED?' Jed clamored.

Slight bafflement from the crowd.

'FOR THEY WHO HAVE *FOR-NI-CAY-TED* CANNOT BLUSH! AS IT SAYS IN THE BOOK OF JEREMIAH ...' Here he took a flicker of a pause as if he knew what was coming.

'Bullfrog!' yelled a voice, sure enough.

Jed tapped the air like an auctioneer acknowledging a bid. It occurred to me there was nothing – no riposte, no joke, no heckle – he'd not heard before. The crowd was an orchestra, and he was playing them like a conductor. 'ARE THEY ASHAMED OF THEIR DETESTABLE BEHAVIOR? NO, THEY HAVE NO SHAME AT ALL! YOU WOMEN ARE GOING TO HELL!'

It was deliberate antagonism and the crowd rose to the bait. They tried to counter him with logic, with outrage, with contradiction.

'"Judge not, lest ye be judged". Isn't that in your book?' someone called.

'DON'T TRY TO *OUT-BIBLE* ME!' Jed shouted back. 'YOU MASTURBATE, SON?'

'Every chance I get!'

'BUT YOU ARE A MAN. WHEN YOU TOUCH YOURSELF, YOU ARE TOUCHING A MAN. WHAT DO YOU CALL THAT, SON?'

No answer. Then from the back of the crowd: 'Syllogism!' That one pretty much went over everyone's head.

'HO-MO-SEXU-ALITY!' cried Jed. 'THERE IS A SPECIAL FIRE IN HELL FOR HOMOSEXUALS. THAT IS NOT A JUDGEMENT, SON. THAT IS A CONDEMNATION.'

A smattering of applause for this. I looked around at the faces of the students. Most were bemused. But a few were resolutely engaged in what he had to say, and that scared me. I remembered what it was like to be eighteen or nineteen, on your own for the first time, susceptible to any tinhorn doctrine that comes along: Carlos Castaneda, Hermann Hesse, transcendental meditation, pot, Baba Ram Dass, Kant, Camus, LSD, Bob Dylan, Kahlil Gibran, didactic prophets coming down from the mountain with tablets of stone. *Be-Jesus-ment* was as powerful a mindfuck as any of that, and this Jed Smock guy knew it. He was a spiritual cradle-robber. When the crowd dispersed, I approached him and asked to talk. I was thinking of writing up a story.

'Of course, brother. I've always got time for recovering addicts.'

'What? I've never been an—'

'Prison?'

'Why are you hassling college kids?'

'As goes the campus, so goes the country. I visit 250 colleges a year. And the message is always the same. "See to it that no one takes you captive by philosophy and empty deceit", Colossians 2:8.'

'They're just *youngsters*. Certainly, the impetus for salvation is adultery, bankruptcy, political disgrace . . . you're in the wrong part of town.'

'"For here the money lenders thrive in their ivory towers".'

'Money lenders?'

'Student loans, son. "You cannot serve God and money", Matthew 6:24.' And so on. It was like trying to reach an extension and getting cycled back to the Operator Jesus.

I went back upstairs to my library table and thought about what I had just seen. The whole event had struck me as extraordinarily electric. And as I replayed it in my head a comical notion occurred: what if it had suddenly been revealed to that crowd – primed as it was for an onslaught from a fevered servant of Lord Jesus Christ himself – that the whole thing was a wind-up, a joke, a *parody* of evangelism? Why, that crowd would have exploded like plankton!

In that instant, everything changed. I had never imagined being a comedian – I couldn't picture myself holding an entire crowd in thrall. But I *could* picture myself pulling the rug out from underneath one.

I went back to my apartment, loaded my belongings into the truck and headed for Missouri.

'Tell me about the job,' Erin said and lit a Salem.

We were at a window table overlooking the Missouri River. You could look outside and see cars crossing the Blanchette Memorial Bridge, which separates St Louis County from St Charles. The restaurant was called Noah's Ark and, indeed, had been built to resemble Noah's Ark. The gimmick was that whatever you ordered, you got two of. Thus, four tired-looking salads, four stale bread rolls and four glasses of synthetic iced-tea were arranged before us.

My job. I was hoping to delay this topic, that we could just enjoy the sheer delight of being in each other's company again. But there it was.

'I imagine you can tell from the hysterical nature of my letters that—'

'What letters?'

'Oh.'

I reached out and flicked the bread roll in front of me, making it spin like a tiny football. When it stopped, I told her I'd quit the newspaper.

'You've *what?*'

'I have no intention of knuckling through life doing something I hate.'

'Then what *do* you intend to do?'

'I'm going to tell you, and you're going to want to break up with me.'

'We *are* broken up, you idiot.'

'That's not official.'

'It doesn't require *paperwork.* I knew you'd show up eventually.'

'If it's all the same to you then, I'd prefer we broke up on my terms.'

'Oh, I see. Well, go ahead.'

'Erin . . .'

'Pass the Thousand Island, will you?'

'Here . . . what is this, *agent orange?* Erin, whatever this race is that I'm scratched from—'

'What race?'

'The horse thing. Your mom—'

'Oh, who cares what my mom says?'

'Well, I do. Stuff like that really gets to me. And I'm here to tell you, I'm withdrawing from that particular race on my own. So, it's now a moot assessment.'

'What is?'

'Whether I make the race or not.'

'Rich, what in God's holy name are you getting at?'

'I'm going to be a comedian.'

She didn't say anything for a moment. Then: 'That's crazy. That's break-up crazy.'

'I knew you'd see it like that. But may I remind you, you're the one who initiated the idea that I should be a misfit—'

'When did I do *that*?'

'Now I intend to follow it through.'

'So you're throwing away your career in journalism?'

'I can't be a misfit *and* a journalist.'

'Hunter S. Thompson is.'

'I'm no Hunter S. Thompson. I can't maintain that prodigious level of self-abuse. I want to do comedy.'

'How do you *do* comedy?'

'You say, "I am a comedian".'

'But don't you need to be able to make people laugh? Normal people?'

'I'm working on that part.' I picked up the menu. 'What are you having?'

'I've lost my appetite,' she said in a way that made me think, *There's still something here.*

She stubbed her cigarette out in a small ceramic ashtray. The ashtray portrayed a pair of monkeys rowing a lifeboat. I guess absurd revisionism was the theme of the evening. Then she stood up and leaned in close. For a second, I thought she was going to kiss me.

'Well, Rich Hall, I hope you meet your calling. I hope you meet the right girl and make a name for yourself. And I sincerely hope you stay away from St Charles, Missouri.'

She was out the door before our four soups even arrived.

*

I drove through Missouri heartbroken. It took me almost 200 miles to mentally reconfigure Erin's remarks into a perfectly agreeable inducement. *Find my calling and make a name for myself, thus effectively restoring Erin's buoyant companionship throughout the known world, save for the town of St Charles, Missouri.* Weren't those her exact words?

It was time to knuckle down.

In Concordia, Missouri, I found a Goodwill and bought a cheap white linen suit and a painting of *Dogs Playing Poker*. In Joplin, Missouri, I found an art supply superstore. And at Kansas State University in Manhattan, I found my calling.

Wichita, Emporia, Lawrence, Tulsa, Norman, Stillwater. How does a comedian get good quickly? Volume! I did five, six shows a day until my throat was as raw and husky as a cornstalk. Every morning I'd go to the local bank and watch the teller empty the change bucket into the hopper and return with crisp bills, then I'd climb in my truck and head out for the rapture of the highway and the next college town.

Denton, Waco, College Station, Austin. The jokes got tighter, the performances got looser. I'd fill up the notebooks with new ideas, fill up on petrol at the all-night truck stop, all those gas pumps lit up like little islands. I stayed at cheap motels, the kind the Gideons Bible people bypassed, with stained bedspreads and carpeting as hideous as Bill Cosby's sweaters. Or, occasionally, I crashed on some sympathetic student's couch, waking up in the detritus of George Carlin and Cheech and Chong LPs, empty pizza boxes, bongs and batik. *The Prophet* by Kahlil Gibran staring at me from a cheap bookshelf. Prophet, my ass.

San Antonio, Houston, Lubbock, El Paso. All that Texas sky and endless road. All the time in the world to conjure new bits or replay the mental game film from the last gig. What went wrong back there in Abilene, were those kids just too uptight or did I choke? Nothing is as profound as bombing, and I anguished after a less-than-stellar gig, trying to surmise what had gone wrong. Audiences don't lie. If it's not funny, they let you know – *boy, do they let you know*. Comedy doesn't bullshit.

Albuquerque, Portales, Española, Las Cruces. 'There's a guy out on the Commons, baptizing dogs!' Campus reporters showed up to interview me. *What have we here?* I never told them my real name. I told them I was the illegitimate son of Jerry Lee Lewis. That I had been a hotwalker for thoroughbreds at Churchill Downs in Kentucky, kicked in the head by a horse named Scratch and found God. That I used to name hurricanes for the National Weather Service and got fired for naming a tropical storm *Juggs*. They wrote all this down with straight, noncommittal faces. The only authentic thing I could say about myself was that I was completely inauthentic. My words were fabricated, and my identity was borrowed, yet comedy felt like the truest thing I'd ever done in my life.

Flagstaff, Tucson, Tempe. At night I dreamt selectively of Erin. I had drawn a line around my future, and I still stupidly believed she could color it in. All she needed was to see this new, defined Rich Hall, this horse who was going to finish. Read into that what you will. I was twenty-three, myopic with infatuation and patently unable to tell the difference between love and 'I told you so'.

*

One evening in Tempe, after a day of shows at Arizona State University, I wandered into a place called Chuy's Choo Choo on Mill Avenue and signed up for the open mike. I knew that if I was going to be a real comedian, I needed to find my own voice, to be more than just a collegiate inside joke. I was beginning to feel like one of those guys who graduates but never leaves.

'What kind of stuff do you play?' the club owner asked. He had a big, walrus moustache and wore flimsy drawstring trousers with the legs rolled up, a sartorial suggestion that he might have once casually thumbed a copy of *Das Kapital*.

'I don't play anything. I do stand-up comedy.'

He looked at me quizzically. 'Where are they all coming from?' he said. I didn't know what he meant by that, nor was I certain the question was even directed at me. He shrugged to himself and wrote my name down on the list.

I bought a beer and shifted down to the end of the bar. The place was your bog-standard folkie pit. Mismatched chairs. Framed photos of singer-songwriters on the walls. Above the stage, someone had stenciled the Dylan lyric 'Yonder stands your orphan with his gun' in small, English uncials. I supposed this was an attempt to thread mortality and time to the music of the spheres. Onstage, a lank-haired twenty-year-old with a black Ovation guitar sat on a stool, murdering James Taylor, his eyes winched so tightly closed it looked like the lyrics were stabbing him a thousand little times. I looked around at the crowd to see if they were buying this – because if they were I was out of there – but they seemed to recognize an emotional scam when they saw one.

I pulled out my notebook and started extracting the bits I thought might work on their own. Nervous? Never. Street performing had made me impregnable. I was so used to building a show from scratch that a ready-made audience seemed like a luxury.

Surprisingly, the next act was a comedian. Or rather, a magician attempting to transition into comedy. He was a strikingly good-looking fellow – darkly complected, cheekbones like an Apache – clearly at ease with himself onstage. The girls in the room fluttered. The guys crossed their arms reflexively. He had a few good jokes and a lot of undercooked ones, which he managed to offset with some adroit sleight-of-hand that recovered the room every time.

He was followed by a very pretty girl with long braided pigtails and an enamel rose behind one ear. We all waited patiently as she made a delicate perch on the stool, repositioned the mike to *just-right-there* and began to twiddle with a complicated open tuning on her guitar, signifying a real opus. Then she proceeded to play the same fucking James Taylor song as the previous guy.

I started writing something in my notebook.

'Who's up for more comedy?' Walrus-Face called out, an amiable-enough emcee.

Modicum of excitement.

'Please welcome, Rich Hall.'

Somnolence of applause.

I stepped up to the mike and unfolded a piece of paper torn from my notebook.

'I have a letter here from James Taylor. *Ahem.* "To whom it may concern. I regret to inform each and every one of you that *you've no longer got a friend* in James Taylor. I know I made a few promises in the past, but too many of you people are taking this shit *way* too seriously. *Put down the guitar and back away.* Do you honestly believe you can just call out my name and, wherever I am, I'll come running to see you again? Like I have super-attenuated hearing, like I'm a *bat*? Use the phone next time, asshole. Or don't. Doesn't matter to me 'cause *I'm not coming.* And another thing. If the sky above you turns dark and full of clouds and that old north wind begins to blow, that's not a sign you need a friend. That's a sign you need a coat. It's called *weather . . .*"'

'Balls,' the magician/comedian said to me afterward. I could feel frost coming off most of the musicians in the room and was enjoying the hell out of it. 'You just said what everyone was thinking. How long you been doing stand-up?'

'Actually, that was my first time on a real stage.'

'Not bad.'

He bought me a beer, and we sat at the back of the club. His name was Bob Dubac. He told me that he had been touring with a band called Sea Level, that they'd headed back to Macon, Georgia, for the Christmas break and dumped him here in Tempe. He drove an Econoline van, said he got his mail at a post office box in Aspen, Colorado. The mention of that town stilled a heart-worn memory in my mind. I knew that town – the Sullivans went there every Easter. They owned a 'chalet': a monstrosity of lodgepole pine and wall-to-wall windows that John T. actually believed could compete with the surrounding mountains for radiance. 'Cowboy mansion,' the locals

34

called it, derisively. Last Easter, when I was still marginally in their graces – when Mr and Missus had acceded to Erin's insistence – I'd stayed there. We had a corner bedroom with a protruding balcony facing the Maroon Bells. We lay in bed and plotted mild indignations against the Sullivan family name. We skied the Snowmass complex, and she taught me how to stem christie. We got hammered on Galena Street. Christ, that seemed like a lifetime ago . . .

Walrus-Face approached Bob and me, spun a chair around and straddled it. He slammed his pint glass hard on the table.

'That stuff about James Taylor,' he said to me, 'does it make you feel big to make other people feel little?'

I flinched at the abruptness of the question.

'Just kiddin' with ya!' He laughed and slapped me on the back. 'You should be here week after week, having to listen to this crap!' He took a swig of beer and swiped his ridiculous moustache with a forearm. 'You fellas local?'

'Road warrior,' Bob replied.

'How's that?'

'The Allman Brothers keep splintering into side-projects, and I'm tasked with entertaining the crowds beforehand while they sit in the dressing room and try to remember each other's names.'

'Rock and roll, brother.'

'I'm a street performer,' I chimed in.

'That's what someone said. Those two over there say they saw you on the commons at ASU today. Pretending to be a preacher man.'

He pointed at two girls chatting earnestly at a table across the room. One of them, a slightly older blonde, looked my way and smiled sunnily while Walrus-Face crooked a finger up and down in mid-air above my head. I felt a flush of self-consciousness and wished I was better dressed. He turned back to us. 'Coupla desperados under the eaves, huh? Tell me, this comedy deal taking off? I'm a little behind the eight ball.'

'Who knows? It's a social experiment,' said Bob. 'America is just one beautiful opportunity after another.' His eyes were tracking the girls' movements.

Walrus-Face laughed. 'Yeah, I used to believe that too.' The girls had gathered their drinks and were heading our way. 'Good luck, fellas,' he said and hauled himself off toward the bar. A real social butterfly, that one.

The girls were grad students. The sunny-faced one, whose name was Cynthia and who hailed from Chicago, said she was studying international finance.

'What's grad school like?' I asked.

'Fine, if you're prepared to give up everything that means anything in your life. This is my first night out in a month.'

'So, no love life?' I felt slightly stricken at my own question.

'Hah! Not a chance. Someday I plan to be reabsorbed into the real world. But not anytime soon. Occasionally I'll get some malleable type to go to bed with me, just to stay in the loop. But they're out with the morning trash. If you get my meaning.'

I did. But it sounded more like she was offering to let me go through her trash.

It was all deeply depressing.

*

Bob hatched a plan: *Piste-Off Comedy.* He said, between now and April, every ski town in Colorado would be heaving with people looking for something to do at night. We could find a venue – a bar, a good-time joint, a small cabaret – promote the shows ourselves and have the run of the place. Ski all day, comedy at night.

'We've got the handicap on the whole shit-heel entertainment game,' he said. 'No instruments, no big sound rigs – just two guys and a mike. Cash and carry.'

I thought it sounded like a great idea. I thought it sounded like the only idea. I went out to the parking lot and stared at my truck with its sagging bumper and doleful-looking, broken headlight. It looked like it was thinking, 'Now what?' I started it up, pulled in behind Bob's Econoline and, together, we hit the Hope–Crosby Road, searching for a hot lead on America's funny bone.

At a bar called Singin' Sadie's Saloon in Breckenridge, the owner said, 'What the hell, comedy, let's give it a shot.' We plastered posters onto all the windows on Main Street and talked up a crowd. By the fifth night of the run, we were filling the room: powder hounds, hippies, Wall Street exiles, old-timers, acid burnouts, assorted social mutants. They were skied out and blissed out and giddy and full of drunken bonhomie, and they took us right under their wings, God bless 'em.

In Steamboat Springs, we set up in a place called Old Town Pub. Christmas lights in the shape of jalapeño peppers draped the stage. Every night, the anomalous ring of beer mugs and big open-throated laughter filled the room. The entire audience looked like it was dressed for some buckaroo-themed costume ball: fringed leather, goose-down vests, sequined denim, snakeskin Tony Lamas – the piety of old-timey days repackaged as Cowboy Hipsterism. One night I peered into the crowd and caught sight of a table of three guys in Stetsons and turtlenecks. *That's just not right*, I thought, *just not right*. It threw me off my rhythm and the after-image burned in my head for days.

Then, Telluride: an old mining town nestled in an imposing box canyon that ascended so operatically it seemed to suggest that, once you got in, you weren't getting out. We played the Victorian saloon at the New Sheridan Hotel, mining laughs the way prospectors a hundred years before had mined silver.

We got funnier. The shows got better. Bob – having ascertained sleight-of-word was far more rewarding than sleight-of-hand – wrote like crazy. As for myself, I was a congestion of fertile ideas – well, sight gags mostly – wired in series like storage batteries. I had a prop case containing a Slinky toy 'Bible', a mocked-up LP album titled *God's Greatest Hits*, a Lacoste polo shirt with a ridiculously oversized alligator sewn to the breast, a tape recorder with a Groucho mask affixed to it that did Johnny Mathis impressions, a suction cup bathtub mat ('squid pelt'), a matchbook cover that read, 'Learn How to Write Pornography in Your Spare Time', and my pièce de résistance: a ski jacket constructed entirely of used lift tickets. Admittedly, unsophisticated stuff, but perfect for ski-crowds who didn't want to have to think too much.

Crested Butte, Arapahoe Basin, Keystone, Winter Park: 'You guys are a riot.'

We were, as they say, *in demand*.

After the shows, any variety of fascinating women could be relied on to chat Bob up – compliant exchanges I observed with no small amount of envy. With his reptilian charm and thin social conscience, he could choose companions the way most of us choose hotels – and for the same reason: a decent bed for the night. I took to grading their looks by chain quality: Ritz-Carltons, Four Seasons, a good number of Marriotts and Hiltons and, to his credit, never anything skankier than a Holiday Inn.

Me, I stayed at ski hostels, cheap and cheerful, reeking of varnish and ambient weed. I lay on my bunk and contemplated the rickety logic of this new life I'd invented. It was joyously uncomplicated. *I got a gig*, I'd say to myself, and felt like an old jazzman.

Aspen. Early April. 1978. She's here. Of that, I'm fairly certain.

The crispness of the air and the Wild West veneer gives this town an extraordinary romance. The surrounding peaks rather specifically rule the skyline. Through every open shop door, the buoyant chiming of cash registers and piping conversation. Skiers and couples and families stroll by, cheerful clusters of contentment, wrapped in fur, emanating abundance.

At the bookstore on Original Street, I browse for too long. I can't concentrate. I'm in that brainless nirvana that makes the world go round and James Taylor write songs. The small Hispanic woman behind the counter finally says, 'Anything in particular?'

'Demented missions of courtship.'

'What other kind is there?'

'Okay. Doomed romance. But in a modestly contemporary vein.'

'Feeling sorry for ourselves, are we?'

'No. It's a gift.'

We settle on *The House of Mirth* by Edith Wharton, and I ask for it to be delivered to Erin, no note. I tell the owner it's the cowboy mansion, the one skiers pass coming down the Eddy Out trail. She shows me a map of Snowmass Village and – because I am having a kind of out-of-body moment – I'm able to recognize the chalet's configuration from an aerial perspective. I draw a circle around it and give her twenty dollars. Later that afternoon, I return and buy *Gravity's Rainbow* by Thomas Pynchon. I scrawl the word *impenetrable* on every one of the first thirty pages. Because it is. I ask for that to be delivered too. The idea is to build up a little humorous intrigue.

The following morning, the owner hands *me* a book: the Rand McNally *Road Atlas*. She crisscrosses her huge forearms high on her chest and watches me read the inscription on the inside: *'Dear Rich. What in the world. Stop this now. Erin.'*

'Did she come in?' I ask.

'Yes. She is exceptionally uncommon. And way out of your league.'

'What would you recommend now?'

'What the atlas implies: leave town.'

I fan all this away, all this sass, this repudiation of chemistry. 'I'm not leaving town,' I say. 'I got a gig.'

Not an hour later, I am standing on skis on a ridge overlooking the Sullivan's lodge. I don't really have a plan, am unsure of what I'm going to do next. Does that make me a stalker? I accept that many a past-life story now owes an apology to the present. But let me emphasize this: *No.* Literature is full of unrequited misfits like me, and they are above censure: Jay Gatsby, Rhett Butler – read your classics! Sure, I don't have Gatsby's sophistication or Rhett's Dixie-fied gallantry. And emotional martyrdom should be represented more strikingly than a guy in possession of rental skis and 143 dollars stuffed in a backpack on a bunk bed at a funky hostel. Still, it's the same basic template: boy meets girl, boy loses girl, boy gets girl back. Give me a break.

The front door opens, and she steps out onto the wraparound deck. She is carrying a pair of 180-centimetre Völkl skis – the ideal cruising length. She steps off the deck, drops the skis into the snow in perfect alignment and locks into the bindings.

I consider swooping down and executing a perfectly edged 180-degree stop in front of her – a spectacular entrance. I could flash my smile and utter something beguiling and perfectly idiotic, something that would instantly crack her up: *Erin. I see that your grandeur has not diminished. Jake's Abbey. Galena Street. Tonight. 9pm.*

She will come to my show, see that I am now a thing of substance, not just a deadbeat clattering through life like a wayward ping-pong ball. *Come with me, Erin. We will ski together high up in the glade of the Maroon Bells at 14,000 feet, where the hares have shed their white winter pelage and flakes of jasper and obsidian glisten in the blinding sunlight. And when spring arrives and the snow has melted away, we will tilt and lurch from these dawn-lit peaks into the gaping maw of Show Business as cannonades of Middle American laughter explode in the sky above our heads like fireworks.*

I am, and always will be, delusional.

The door opens a second time, and a man emerges. I'm a little surprised because I didn't think John T. Sullivan was a skier. Then I realize it's not John T. Sullivan. It's a younger man, cutting an athletic stride across the porch, flamboyant in a golden-hued ski suit with brocade down the sides. *Brocade!*

Who the hell is this clown? He sidles up to Erin and, astonishingly, throws an arm around her shoulder in a way that indicates all he wished for in his mind's eye is now happening. She responds with just the slightest tell-tale bump of her hip against his groin. I feel sick.

I stand and watch as the two of them take off, planing downhill in tranquil zigzags, carving perfect quotation marks. Eventually they become small mutual figures. But Erin's form stays unmistakable. I know she and this jackass will head for the abandon of the black diamond trails, the ones with names like *Howler, Wildcat* and *Grinder*. Me, I'm relegated to the green runs and their appropriate nomenclature: *Galavant, Dawdler, Lunchline*. Same mountain, wildly different paths.

Years later, when I was a fully-formed comedian (and fully insured), we would run into each other, and she would confide that her brief marriage to the erstwhile academic and flamboyant imbecile, E.J. Thrift, was the biggest mistake she had made in a life otherwise short on regrets. She told me she was proud of me for what I'd done with my own. I smiled politely and resisted the urge to say, 'I told you so.' At heart, I am a Southerner, where graciousness still counts for something.

CHAPTER 2

QUANDO

The Tick Tock Diner sprawls alongside Route 3 in Clifton, New Jersey. It looks like someone from the 1940s' idea of a space colony, all glass and chrome, a relic of the past trying to predict the future. Its most notable feature is a looming preposterous clock, exhorting travelers to *Eat Heavy* in six-foot-high lettering.

I used to emcee a *Gong Show*-themed showcase there every Tuesday night. This was back in the early eighties, when I was living in Passaic, New Jersey, and gigging late at night in Manhattan, a straight shot up Route 3. The show, which paid $25, was staged in a backroom function hall with forlorn carpeting and an angry-looking chandelier. It was populated by wretched local talent, but there was one act – General George A. Custer – who killed me every time. The General, true to his namesake, sported a fringed buckskin coat and knee-high rawhide boots. His shoulder-length blond tresses seemed incongruous – too youthful-looking for the hard, lined face they

45

accompanied. His *specialty*, for lack of a better word, was singing to a backing track of the Engelbert Humperdinck song 'Quando, Quando, Quando'.

I would announce, 'Ladies and Gentlemen, General George Armstrong Custer!' and the crowd, possessing a special bloodlust for the poor guy, would bray. The General was oblivious to all this. He would stride onstage with a haughtiness that suggested all prior entertainment was an insult to his presence. Raising a gloved finger, he would demand silence, then cue whoever was in charge of the backing track. There was always a flurry of surreptitious betting on how many *quandos* the General could get through before being unceremoniously gonged. Serious money changed hands during that interval.

I marveled at the man. What kind of guy, I wondered, wakes up every Tuesday morning knowing, no matter how spectacular his day goes, it's going to end in '. . . tell me Quando, Quando . . .' *CLAAAANG!!* – and *still* comes back the following Tuesday?

Who knows what drove him? Perhaps a self-loathing that craved being deliciously humiliated. But I wanted to believe the guy carried a flame. A flame of tenacity. A flame that wouldn't extinguish until the day it burned – *quandos* intact – through every verse and chorus of that insipid song. In this I found a kind of reverse inspiration. I was still fairly new to comedy – a weed breaking through concrete. When Bob Dubac and I had started out, there was no roadmap for comedians, just a roadmap over the next hill. But we'd both realized soon enough that making strangers laugh crowded out everything else in our lives, so he'd headed for LA. I chose the East Coast. It felt grittier. I was a pretty good comic, but I had no true voice yet, no presence that transcended my material, no comedic afterglow. In other words, I didn't know yet who I was *supposed* to be, and that was daunting. But I knew who I *wasn't* supposed to be, and that was General George A. Custer.

The Texas musician Ray Wylie Hubbard once explained, via verse: *'There's two kinds of people in the world. The day people and the night people. And it's the night people's job to get the day people's money.'* The purest description of show business, if ever there was one.

My day started when most hardworking folks were turning in for bed. I would drive up Route 3 into the maw of the Lincoln Tunnel, glide beneath the Hudson River for a sonorous mile-and-a-half and emerge into the glaring throb of midtown Manhattan. I had a 1971 Volkswagen Squareback that had broken down so many times I could probably have reassembled it blindfolded, like a soldier and his M16. I would park the thing near Times Square and hoof a half-dozen blocks to the Improv at West 44th and 9th Avenue to do a twenty-minute spot.

Everything about Midtown Manhattan was sleazy and startling, like it had been painted onto black velvet. And that, to me, was its appeal. You could look into the anomie and see possibilities. New Jersey, with its graceless commuter sprawl, offered nothing but a narcosis of non-inspiration. It seemed to me if I lived in Manhattan, I could awaken every morning to the unpredictable: a wondrous stewpot of petty crime, whores, pimps, Billy Joel, big hair, Jordache jeans, swinging medallions, Billy Joel, boom boxes, *A Chorus Line*,

Studio 54, crack cocaine, smack, potholes, Billy Joel, and the gagging stench of what New Yorkers call *overflowing sanitation* and the rest of the country calls *raw garbage*. Why, the jokes would practically write themselves!

Few of us floundering comedians could afford to live in Manhattan. We drifted in from the margins like fruit pickers in a Steinbeck novel, harvesting laughs. Jerry Seinfeld tooled in from Queens. Larry Miller took the B train from Flatbush. Carol Leifer came in from Sheepshead Bay. Some comics would drive all the way down from Boston or up from Philadelphia, knock out a spot at the Improv, then sleep in their cars. We converged after our sets at the backroom bar, amid the fug of cigarette smoke and stale beer. We polished jokes, dissected routines, conjugated half-formed premises, somehow believing comedy was a componential thing, like a beryllium sphere. We nattered about the *deal* that was in the works, the agent who was *interested*, the unattainable waitress, the unreliable road conquest. Everything was imaginable. We were a herd of steers, heads under the fence post, clawing at the good stuff that was right . . . over . . . there.

Steve Martin was filling stadiums. George Carlin's albums had gone platinum. *Saturday Night Live* was in its ascendancy and, significantly, NBC had announced it was bringing a live ninety-minute morning comedy talk show to New York, hosted by David Letterman. Letterman's snarky, irreverent disdain for the contrivances of television could only mean this was going to be something remarkably abnormal.

Budd Friedman owned the Improv. He'd bought it in 1963 with

the idea of establishing a watering hole for comedians and actors. Previously, it had been a Vietnamese restaurant, and when Budd pulled down the coverings, he found a red brick wall. That's where he put the stage. Had he not had that foresight, the bulk of today's comics would be performing in front of a tapestry of lotus blossoms. Budd presided over the place with an arrogant self-regard that belied the fact he had no discernible talents. He was the only living person I'd ever known to wear a monocle.

One busy Saturday night in June, I arrived to find him seated at his usual corner table under an array of framed 8x10s. Budd had lined the Improv's walls with comedians he imagined having nurtured: Robin Williams, David Brenner, Robert Klein, Elayne Boosler, Andy Kaufman, Elaine May, Mike Nichols, Shelley Berman. Desperate to convey *funny*, their faces seemed frozen in a tortured rictus. Only the pop-eyed, catatonic Rodney Dangerfield looked like his natural self, assuming you considered pop-eyed catatonia to be a natural state.

Budd was sipping the house champagne. (I'd tasted it once and, let me tell you, those were some tough little grapes.) There was a pile of receipts and food and beverage forms on the table that he seemed to be striving to ignore.

'Mr Hall, Mr Hall,' he called out with theatrical articulation. 'I need a word with you.'

'What's up, Budd?'

Like something off the cover of *The New Yorker*, he inserted his monocle to signify eminence. 'I'm putting together a showcase for Letterman's people next Thursday, to which I've added your name. Can you appreciate that?'

'That sounds great.' In truth, I felt a flux of mild panic. This was a Big Deal.

'Eight minutes, tight,' he instructed. 'Bring your A material and don't screw it up. I say this knowing it all may be well out of reach for you.'

'Thanks, Budd,' I said and abruptly walked away. I suppose some token demonstration of fealty to the man had been expected, but I was in kind of a daze. *Letterman.*

I wandered somewhat absent-mindedly into the showroom, compressed myself against a wall and watched the room filling up. Usually before a show, I liked to gauge the room's vibe. But I couldn't concentrate. Budd's offer rankled me, probably because, as much as I *loved* comedy, I *hated* show business: showcases, auditions, the desperate skiting for validation, the false modesty, the hoary sentimentality of *big breaks* and *once-in-a-lifetime opportunities.* It struck me as glorified beggary. At this very moment, around the corner at the Schubert Theatre, louche thespians were lock-stepped in a chorus line of nightly supplication: *God, I hope I get it . . . I really need this job . . . I've got to get this job . . .*

I despised that kind of bullshit. So, because I liked to think I was the furthest thing from insecure, I conjured up a sort of inner bravado – an attitude that was less 'Letterman: Big Deal', more 'letterman: big deal' – and distracted myself by eavesdropping on a Long Island-type couple at a nearby table.

'This show better be a pisser,' the girl was saying in a voice that sounded like a stiletto. She had alarming shoulder pads, like she'd been upholstered. A harried-looking waitress appeared with leafy cocktails, juleps of some kind. The girl slid back in her chair and clasped her hands in amazement as if the drinks were some exotic species of birdlife. Her lubricious boyfriend eyed this exchange with casual disdain. The ridiculous flare of his jacket collar mimicked an equally ridiculous shirt collar so that he resembled a cormorant emerging from an oil slick. Pre-show music pulsed through the room. Whoever programmed it had decided that, in the prevailing climate with disco and adult-oriented rock at loggerheads, Billy Joel was the man to bridge the divide.

'I *love* this song!' the girl squealed and began ululating. Stylistically speaking, New York City in 1980 had lost its mind.

The show that night featured two notable incidents. Larry David, who perpetually carried the onstage demeanor of an old man rudely awakened from a nap, stormed offstage after six minutes. His set was generating little more than polite torpor and, when the julep girl suddenly emitted a big honking sneeze in the middle of his delivery, he stopped and glared at her.

'Why would you sneeze over my punchline?' His head was tilted quizzically to one side. The girl looked around the room helplessly. 'Who *does* that?' Larry demanded. 'Who comes to a comedy show and sneezes over the punchlines?'

'Those were *punchlines*?' someone intoned from the dark. The microphone began to writhe in Larry's hand. At this point, several comedians from the adjoining bar had darted into the showroom to see what minor grievance had ignited his emetic rage. I think we all got the feeling he was looking for an excuse to escape. Julep girl let loose with another violent spasm, a high-velocity snot rocket that moved a couple's hair at an adjacent table.

'*What the hell is wrong with you, lady?*' Larry seethed. The boy-friend made a half-hearted attempt to speak up for her.

'She's allergic to mint,' he explained. You could see they were embarrassed but Larry wouldn't let up.

'Are you trying to *infect* me? What if I came to your salon and sneezed all over your tanning bed, you stupid woman!' He glared around the room as if our accumulated presence was an affront to his hygiene, then said: 'You know what? Screw you people!'

He chucked the mike to the floor and strode off, his hands raised in a kind of invocation. I watched him disappear into the bar and said to myself, *That guy is not cut out for comedy.* (A misjudgment that would eventually rival my dad's assessment of the British Invasion: 'Trust me, once all the dust has settled, Petula Clark will be bigger than the Beatles.')

Later in the show, as I was about to go on, Budd pulled me aside. 'The delightful Ms Eydie Gormé is with us. She's headlining the Starlite Outdoor Theater with Steve Lawrence tomorrow night. Take a moment onstage to honor her presence, would you?'

'Yeah, sure,' I replied emptily. Steve and Eydie were one of those Vegas acts who swoop onstage, plant themselves like plastic wedding cake figures and proceed to sing at each other. Not my kind of music, and not my kind of crowd.

I went onstage, launched into my set, and forgot about Eydie until I saw Budd outlined in the bar doorway, gesturing eagerly toward the back of the room. I paused mid-sentence. 'Oh, by the way,' I announced, 'we have a special guest tonight: Ms Eydie Gormé, ladies and gentlemen!'

A great beacon of spotlight bathed the back of the room, revealing a seated kimono-encrusted Ms Gormé. She rose to her feet like a resurrection. In terms of sheer wattage, her blinding alabaster teeth gave the spotlight a run for its money. There was a general craning of necks and robust applause. Eydie threw a confectionary kiss at the crowd and sat back down. The name of the venue she was appearing at had escaped me so, instead, I said, 'God only knows what physical horrors lurk beneath that kimono!'

I don't know where that came from.

There was an audible gasp from some of the crowd. Others guffawed. I supposed I'd split the room on that one and cruised through the rest of my set to mixed appreciation. It didn't matter. I felt exhilarated. What Larry had done to the julep couple struck me as callous. They were just everyday people, entitled to an evening of comedy to relieve the tedium of day-to-day existence. Eydie Gormé, on the other hand, was a celebrity. You get what you deserve.

Afterward, I went into the bar and saw Budd making a beeline for me, monocle popping out of his eye socket.

'Mr Hall, we have a strict policy here of not eviscerating celebrities.'

'I'll remember that, Budd.' I shot out the door into the New York night. The air was humid, and Manhattan stank. On every corner, a veritable bouncy castle of rubbish, bursting at the seams. I, on the other hand, was bursting with optimism. I thought to myself: *I may not be right for Letterman's show, but Letterman's show is right for me.* Did we not share a similar contempt for the whole fatuous enterprise? Show business gorged itself on consumption, artifice, the big reveal, the fake surprise. It was 96 percent a wasteland. I spent 23 hours and 40 minutes of my day doing nothing. We were perfect for each other.

A succession of yellow cabs and black town cars crawled the streets like one long mangrove snake. Everywhere, the incessant bleat of horns: a tone-deaf symphony tuning up. If *The Letterman Show* rejected me, it was because I simply wasn't good enough, and I was going to have to bend to the work at hand and get funnier. But, if they hired me, I was going to have to bend to the work at hand and get funnier. The city made everything rational. God, I wanted to live here!

I crossed the clogged 9th Avenue, picking my way through the gaps between car bumpers, amazed at the trust one puts in New Yorkers. One slip of a clutch could render you legless. I thought: *If I lived here, I could ditch my shitty car.* A taxi slammed its brakes in front of me. The driver leaned out his window and delivered an invective in an utterly impenetrable foreign dialect. I thought: *If I lived here, I could sample the cuisines of all nations.*

I reached the other side of the avenue, where a homeless man slouched against a telephone booth. In the yellow reflection of taxis, his face had the pallor of a stubbed-out ashtray. He held up a plastic-bound phone directory and waved it in my general direction. 'Wanna buy the Manhattan *Yellow Pages*?'

I felt subsumed by the sheer human volume of New York. It trivialized all problems, elevated all dreams. I decided: *I will nail this Letterman audition.*

The following Tuesday night, the General came onstage at the Tick Tock Diner to ensnare himself once again in the freeze-frame of despair. Even as I was introducing him, one of the talent show's judges – a local morning drive-time radio motormouth – had deftly raised the rubber mallet and sat there poised to strike. The General never had a chance. The judge let him reach the second refrain of 'Quando' before, assailed by the crowd's malevolence, he delivered the death knell. The General thundered off, shooting me a penetrating glare that intimated this was all somehow my fault. I rushed up onstage and hastily introduced the next act, as if what we had just witnessed had never happened.

I couldn't quite put my finger on what was so mesmerizing about this debacle. Maybe it was the General's wild eyes staring out of his taut face, his absurd costume, the weirdly effete way he would begin shimmering like a dervish to the song's overture, then launch into the vocals with Olympian faith only to be stymied yet again. He was the living embodiment of Wile E. Coyote, and that gong may as well have had 'Acme' written on it.

The show finished shortly afterward. I was due for a late spot at the Improv, so I collected my twenty-five dollars and went out to my car. The air was rank with effluvium from the power plant over in the Meadowlands. The plant sent its electricity to New York City, but the methane stayed in New Jersey.

A gold-colored Pontiac Trans Am – the vehicle of choice for Midwestern rednecks and Vietnam vets – was parked beside my VW. Sleek and rounded like a bicep, it had a turbo-scoop and a great spreadeagle stenciled on the hood. The open driver's door revealed the General, his posture collapsed, cigarette clenched furiously in his teeth. The car's interior overflowed with detritus: clothing, books, newspapers, a carton of Winstons, piles of eight-track tapes. A pair of dog tags dangled from the rear-view mirror. The General looked up and caught me eyeballing him. For some reason I felt like I should console the guy.

'Don't take it too personally, hey?' I said.

He gazed around the parking lot. People were filtering toward their cars, still percolating, no doubt, from the degradation they'd heaped upon him. 'How *am* I supposed to take it?'

'I'm curious how you can go up there week after week and subject yourself to abuse.'

'It takes me out of my own head.'

'You military?'

'Ex.'

'Vietnam?'

'That's what they tell me.'

'Well,' I said, somewhat deferentially, 'thanks for your service to the country.'

'That's a platitude, son.'

'Do you mind if I give you some advice?'

He swung around suddenly, a whorl of fringe, leather and ridiculous buttons. His rangy frame filled the car door opening. 'In what capacity?'

'Well, I'm a stand-up comedian—'

'You coulda fooled me.'

'—and I don't think you're doing yourself any favors by singing "Quando" over and over.'

He stomped his cigarette into the pavement and stared at me

confoundedly. When he finally spoke, it was in the measured tone of someone indulging a simpleton: 'Well, what *other* song can you imagine General George A. Custer singing? The man's romantic liaisons with Native American women are well documented, particularly Quando, the illegitimate daughter of the Cheyenne chief Little Rock and by all accounts an exceedingly comely squaw. Read your history books, son!'

'I guess the problem is I can't imagine General Custer singing at all.'

He took a step forward, gathering erudition. 'The historical depiction of Custer – that is, the one that graces history books, not to mention Adam's otherwise stirring panorama currently residing in the boardroom of the Anheuser-Busch Company in St Louis – portrays him wielding a saber. Rifle in one hand, saber in the other. A blatant historical fallacy. No one in the Seventh Cavalry carried a saber. You follow?'

'No. Not at all.'

'If we are to dispense with historical accuracies altogether, then who's to say Custer didn't have a lovely singing voice?'

'Fair enough point,' I conceded. For fear of further enraging the man, I opted not to inform him that 'quando' was hardly an historical reference, merely the Spanish word for *when*. 'Look, personally I *like* what you're doing. It's like performance art. But I don't think the audience gets it. They've kind of turned it into their little game, and they're mocking you.'

He made a bilious swallowing gesture.

'Well, that is my travail, isn't it? For your information, you impertinent little shit, this isn't the only place I appear. There's an open mike over in Montclair every Thursday at The Frolic Room, including various tryout nights, amateur shows – what have you – up and down the Garden State Parkway. On each of those occasions, my performance meets with vigorous approval. Not unlike the great man himself, whose successes at Washita and French Creek are generally overshadowed by his unfortunate setback at Little Bighorn. This,' he said, indicating the Tick Tock, 'is *my* Little Bighorn.'

'Is that pretty much all you do then? Go onstage and sing "Quando"?'

'Admittedly, it's a limited repertoire,' he replied. 'I could probably do a passable Dennis Hopper' – he raised both hands to mime imaginary Harley handlebars, à la *Easy Rider* – 'but I don't much care for the man's politics. What's performance art?'

'I don't know. *Performance* art. Weird. Unpredictable.'

'Weird? "Quando, Quando, Quando" is an allegory, son. A fallen war hero pining for the parting caress of his forbidden mistress.'

'If you say so.'

'And it's in the key of C, which is in my wheelhouse. Now let me give *you* some advice and listen up hard.' He thrust a gloved finger into my chest. 'Henceforth, I'd like a more dignified stage introduction. Stop trotting me out there like some kind of novelty act.'

He turned toward his car, indicating he was done with this discussion. I left the diner and headed east on Route 3 toward Manhattan.

That the General was unhinged was obvious, but why? Vietnam? History? Show business? It wasn't unusual to meet ex-military types bristling with static. But they didn't, as far as I know, like to dress up as Indian War generals and belt out Humperdinck standards to an audience of jackals. Maybe he was traumatized. Maybe it was a form of therapy.

I passed Giants Stadium where Jimmy Hoffa was purportedly interred beneath the visitors' end zone, a notion that never failed to humor me. You could imagine ol' Jimmy, bug-eyed and squirming in his captor's grip, realizing he was about to become an eternal doormat for a succession of 250-pound NFL wide receivers. At that very moment, a car abruptly pulled up behind me and flashed its brights, blinding me. I thought it must be a cop and tried to check my speedometer, but the high beams were so intense, I could only see my knuckles glaring on the steering wheel.

The car hugged my bumper momentarily, then shot alongside, all chrome and headlights. It was the Trans Am. The General, window down, palomino mane aflutter, held a fresh cigarette in his teeth. He was still wearing his coat and gloves in some kind of defiance of the sweltering night, and he looked like an old mural in a government building. He glanced over at me and, with a well-practiced nonchalance, shifted into turbo-charge and rocketed past, utilizing seventy-five years of GM automotive advancement to convey the message *fuck you*.

What happened next struck me as a bit overly demonstrative. The back of the Trans Am began to shimmy, then jerked wildly. The car went into a protracted spin, flipped upside down, performed a stunning balletic glissade and came to a stop by a guard rail.

That this entire spectacle seemed to be performed solely for my amusement was a notion I quickly put aside. I pulled my car over to the shoulder lane, leapt out and raced toward the wreckage. Clothing and eight-track tapes were strewn everywhere. The underside of the Trans Am lay exposed like a great metallic thorax. Twin shafts of headlight splayed into the sky and music wafted from the car's custom speakers. The General emerged from the driver's window larvally, stood up, brushed at his coat and gazed around.

'Well, *that'll* clear your sinuses,' he said absently.

'Are you okay?'

'I've been in worse dust-ups.'

'What were you trying to prove? You coulda killed both of us driving like that!'

'Goddamn Positraction has got a mind of its own,' he replied, by way of an explanation. He eyed the wreckage with a kind of all-purpose disappointment as if the car had betrayed him, then he reached out a hand and laid it casually on the upended undercarriage. 'They don't make 'em like this anymore, son. That may be a generational judgement, but I seriously doubt it.'

I'd read somewhere that an addiction to daredevilry was one of the ways post-traumatic stress disorder manifested itself. None of the words you'd associate with a car crash – *daze, shock, confusion, trauma* – were evident in him. If anything, he was invigorated. He scrambled a cigarette from his coat pocket and began strolling around the vehicle.

'Follow me, GI,' he commanded, and, for some reason, I did. His hands were clasped behind his back like an old horse trainer at dawn admiring a dewy pasture. The lush tempo drifting up from beneath the car – The 5th Dimension's 'One Less Bell to Answer' – gave the otherwise horrific scenario a detached, easy-listening ambiance.

'When I first shipped out to Nam,' he maundered, 'there was no greater marvel than the mechanical hardware at our disposal. Tanks, halftracks, personnel carriers, Humvees, A310s ... Everything precision-engineered to repel anti-rockets and mortars, all courtesy of Mr John Q. Taxpayer. And, don't you know, we trashed it all! Knocked the tracks off tanks! Smashed personnel carriers! Left Hueys crumpled in some godforsaken culvert like beer cans.'

He turned to me. 'The one thing metal is not fabricated to withstand, son' – here, he raised a finger – 'is adrenalin.'

I didn't know how to respond to any of this. I was now certain he was crazy, so I just said, 'You should probably turn that music off. You don't wanna kill your battery.'

He stared at me blankly.

'That was a joke,' I explained.

'Oh, funny man ... I forgot. I got a joke for you: how many Vietnam vets does it take to screw in a lightbulb? You don't know? Of course you don't. *Cause you weren't there, man! YOU FUCKING WEREN'T THERE!'*

This caught me completely off guard. I've never laughed so hard at a joke while, at the same time, thinking, *I seriously need to get the hell away from this guy.*

By this time, a half-dozen vehicles had skidded to a stop, dispersing a small crowd of onlookers. To make myself useful, I stepped out into the roadway and deployed a kind of 'nothing-to-see-here' choreography to wave them on. I realized I'd somehow managed to entwine myself with an individual who radiated a lifetime of trouble. All I really wanted at that moment was to be onstage at the Improv, cosseted by a crowd. And to forget any of this had happened.

A state trooper arrived and, several minutes later, an ambulance. There was a brief exchange of protestations in which I distinctly heard the General assuring the trooper he would be fine once the artillery subsided in his head. Eventually, he allowed himself to be ushered into the back of the ambulance, which sped off into the night. All that was left was the smell of gasoline and an air of diminished excitement. A few of the onlookers, disappointed at the absence of severed limbs and blood, had shifted their attention to the football stadium looming reverentially in the distance. They chatted among themselves in hushed tones, reliving glorious gridiron memories. A tow truck wheeled up, and everyone drifted off to their cars.

I walked back to my VW, mentally curating the titles of the eight-track tapes scattered in the roadway: *Mel Tormé*; *Marching Music for All Occasions*; *Glen Campbell's Greatest Hits*; *The Best of Dusty Springfield*. I spotted a green fatigue jacket lying in the shoulder and picked it up. Above the right pocket were stenciled the words *A. Vickery*. Seeing the General's real name brought him from the past into the moment. There was a yellow patch on the sleeve: a bisecting bar with a stallion's head above it and a bold Cyrillic number 7. *Fucking Seventh Cavalry*, I thought, which – given the antics I'd just witnessed – went a long way toward explaining why we lost in Vietnam.

I threw the jacket in the back seat of the VW and headed for Manhattan.

*

Unlike the weekend, the Tuesday night Improv line-up was generally of room-temperature quality: a succession of pedestrian, inter-changeable comedians. An anthropologist, viewing stand-up for the first time, would have been surprised by how many had so recently broken up with their girlfriends, though after several disclaimers and professions of personal shortcomings, it became apparent why. An equal number had issues with roommates who failed to respect individually labelled items in the refrigerator. Their punchlines often employed a single descriptive detail followed by an emotive action. 'Funyuns and masturbation', for example. They seemed to spend a lot of time imagining famous celebrities in mundane jobs. They were uniformly dubious of astrology. A good number of the comediennes appeared preoccupied with their own vaginas to which they attrib-uted vastly exaggerated claims, often anthropomorphic in nature. Having been invited to examine a few of these first hand, I found they seldom lived up to the hype.

Fortunately, on this Tuesday, a handful of A-listers had shown up to trial-run their Letterman showcases. As I waited my turn, the sense of what I was up against became increasingly apparent. Carol Leifer, who never talked about her vagina, savaged pop culture like a delicate sniper: 'Linda McCartney playing the keyboards: Red . . . green . . . blue . . . red.' Larry Miller had a routine called 'The Five Stages of Drinking', which was the benchmark for every lugubrious inebria-tion story ever told. He was consummate, every word and gesture lucidly honed. Ronnie Shakes fired precision one-liners: 'Sometimes I wish I was the last man on earth so I could find out how many of those girls were lying.' Jerry Seinfeld, already the exalted everyman of observation, spun gold from Pop-Tarts to pajama pockets. No one could wring more from the flimsiest of premises, or as artfully. Larry David, when he wasn't self-sabotaging, exhibited the same meticulous attention to detail as Seinfeld. It's just that his premises were far more obtuse. On this night, he offered up a disquisition on *rear* admirals and bosun's *mates*. The crowd nodded but forgot to laugh. That was the difference between Jerry Seinfeld and Larry David: Seinfeld built ships in bottles, Larry built ships in cans.

I followed Larry and managed to revitalize the crowd, bounded confidently through my eight minutes and came offstage thinking I was no better or worse than my companions. And therein was the problem: *We were all good.* It was like those movie scenes where the dicey gun dealer shows up with the suitcase and flips it open to reveal a multitude of firepower. '.44 Magnum, real monster. Too much for you? Try this .38 Special. Hell of a wallop. Maybe this is more your style: Walther PK, beautiful little gun, stop an elephant . . .'

I left the club, walked back through Times Square and mentally threw my eight minutes of comedy into the gutter. What good was care and selection if we were *all* careful and selective? I needed something that was bursting at the seams. Something that would make the Letterman people sit up and bark.

I reached my car, which, in its current state of dilapidation, looked about as uncertain as I felt. I unlocked it and, climbing in, noted the fatigue jacket in the back seat. The jacket went with the night, and the night went with the situation and I said to myself: *What do you bring to a gunfight? Answer: a grenade.*

*

On Thursday night, the emcee Joe Piscopo was about to introduce the next showcase comedian when he heard a loud knocking. A door at the side of the Improv stage opened out onto West 44th Street. Now and then, tramps and junkies would bang on it, possibly thinking it was some kind of portal to the mother ship. Piscopo ignored the banging. But when it continued, he politely excused himself to the crowd and went over to open it. The crowd watched his muffled exchange with an unseen voice. 'Sir, I think you've got the wrong location.'

Suddenly, a pizza delivery man pushed past Piscopo, stepped onto the stage and peered curiously out at the audience. He wore a white paper hat, the folding kind you see in fast-food kitchens. Also, an army fatigue jacket. Behind him, Piscopo discreetly stepped out of the spotlight, effectively giving the man ownership of the room.

'Who ordered a 16-inch pepperoni with olives?' the man demanded, raking his gaze from one table to another. He held the pizza box unsteadily, as if it were a hot cannonball. A scattering of laughs from the audience, either from the incongruity of the moment or from an innate foreknowledge that something impromptu was afoot.

'Look folks, I don't know what ya'll got goin' on here,' he said. 'Maybe one of them NuYoRican poetry slams or what have you. But I have a *duty* . . . to deliver and collect on this pizza.'

A few comics and industry-types who had been lounging in the bar area poked their heads into the showroom, sensing something was about to detonate. The man – me, of course – stepped off the stage and into the crowd resolutely, with no idea yet where this was headed. It might be inspired. It might be career suicide.

A young couple sat at the table nearest the stage. The girl's eyebrows were elevated, unsure what was happening, as if the purchase price of a ticket had somehow guaranteed distance between audience and performer.

I looked at the boyfriend. 'You know anything about *duty,* son?'

'Duty?'

'*Duty!* An unstinting commitment to life, liberty and domestic tranquility. What branch did you serve in?'

'I didn't . . .'

I leaned in, turning the side of my head to his face. 'I'm sorry. Could you repeat that answer directly into my one working ear?'

'I'm a student.'

'Where?'

'Nassau Community College.'

'Ohhhhh!' I snapped to a military poise and gave him a thoroughly obsequious salute. 'Thank you for your service to the country, sir.'

Nassau Community College was a dubious diploma mill in nearby Long Island. The calculated local reference tipped the room into laughter. This was starting to take off.

'*Daddy* got him out of the draft!' I shouted. 'I reckon anybody'd dodge the draft would dodge out on paying for a pizza.' I looked back down at him. 'I'm going to ask you one more time, son: *Did you order a 16-inch pepperoni pizza!*'

'No, sir!'

'*With olives!*'

'*No sir!*' He was laughing now.

For someone who didn't want to be the General, I was doing a pretty good job of inhabiting him. Or, rather, inhabiting his jacket to which I had ascribed a history I knew nothing of and a character I had no hope of understanding. I was just freewheeling. But the crowd was going with it, swiveling in their seats, following the tangent.

I drifted to another table: two guys, preppie types. One wore a white Lacoste knit shirt.

'What's that on your shirt, son? Looks like a saltwater crocodile.'

'Alligator,' the guy corrected.

'Same thing. The Mekong River was full of them things. Ever seen what a saltwater crocodile can do to a grunt's leg? You're just sitting in that murky water cooling your feet cause its stinking hot in the jungle, just mindin' your own business, maybe hummin' a Creedence Clearwater song and *chomp*! Takes your big toe right off your foot. Saw it happen to my buddy.' I leaned in for emphasis. '*My buddy gave his big right toe for America's freedom!* And *you* got the nerve to sit there with a crocodile on your chest and *mock* me?'

Full-tilt laughter. God knows where any of this was coming from. Adrenalin, I suppose. But I knew where it was going. By now I'd reached the back of the showroom and the table I'd been targeting all along: Letterman's people. Six, maybe seven of them. The only way I can think of to describe their collective reaction to this performance was *forensically amused*, except for the woman seated at the table's end, who stood out strikingly. She had a wonderfully opaque face and jet-black hair cut into a severe fringe.

'What about you, ma'am? You order this pizza?'

'I don't believe so,' she said.

I set the pizza down, perched on the corner of the table, let silence hang in the air for a moment, then launched into something that resembled a bad audition piece for *Apocalypse Now*.

'Every night, ma'am, I sit in the doorway of my trailer with my Pall Malls and my wine and my Bible. And I stare out at the lightning bugs. You ever watch lightning bugs, ma'am?'

'We call them fireflies,' she replied shrewdly, as if none of this overacting was above her suspicion.

'I loved lightning bugs when I was a kid. Collected 'em in a jar beside my bed. You know what color a jar of lightning bugs makes, ma'am?'

'Why do you keep calling me *ma'am*?'

'Innocence. The color of innocence. Like nothing in this world can ever hurt you. But now when I see lightning bugs, you know what they remind me of?'

'I'm going to guess something unspeakably traumatic.'

I bolted upright from the chair.

'Tracer rounds! Incoming! I'm outta fucking ammo! For the last time . . . who ordered this damn pizza?'

Unfazed by these histrionics, the woman calmly posed a question to me: 'If you had your feet in the Mekong River, why would you have been attacked by a saltwater crocodile?'

'What?'

'The Mekong River would be *freshwater*, wouldn't it?'

It was a perfectly reasonable question that had no business being asked in this kind of car-wreck scenario. I could feel the heat of expectation from the audience. *Stay in character*, I told myself. *Stay in character*. I squinted at her and said: 'I don't know ma'am. Maybe it was an invasive species. I didn't have time to think about it 'cause I was worried about getting my head blown off by an even *more* invasive species. THE FUCKING VIET CONG!'

The audience erupted into applause. The woman, whose name was Merrill Markoe, wasn't at all admonished by the putdown. In fact, she was thinking, *I am considering hiring this man to write on a network comedy show.*

Nearby, partially obscured beneath a slack Yankees baseball cap, sat Letterman, his chair tilted against the wall, hands clasped across his chest – an insouciant posture that suggested he might be enjoying this immensely. I sauntered over to him.

'Oh, it's David Letterman. Famous comedian. I got a joke for you . . .'

The crowd, sensing some sort of brazen confrontation, went absolutely quiet. I had a fleeting terror of things backfiring.

'How many Vietnam vets does it take to screw in a lightbulb?'

The following Tuesday night, I arrived at the Tick Tock and informed the promoter that I had been hired to write on *The David Letterman Show* and this would be my last night as emcee. I went looking for the General and found him behind the curtained-off area that passed for backstage, warming up his voice while smoking a cigarette so intensely it looked like his face hurt. I made a kind of presentational gesture with his jacket, which I'd folded like an American flag.

'Appreciative, son,' he said gruffly. Nothing in his manner acknowledged the previous Tuesday's carnage, and I didn't feel the need to inform him my own fortunes had turned on that jacket, as well as a joke that, depending on one's understanding of the gradations of the term *thievery*, I'd stolen from him.

The show started and, when his turn came to be introduced, I said to the crowd, 'Ladies and gentlemen. The act I'm about to bring up fought for you assholes in Vietnam. Try to bear that in mind. *Please welcome General George Armstrong Custer.*'

The General strutted onto the stage and gave me a look that let me know he saw right through all of this. But there was no braying. No wagering. Instead, a slow, appreciative clap that gained in intensity. He tore through the entire song to a thunderous ovation. To be honest, he had a lovely singing voice. It wasn't Engelbert. But it wasn't bad.

Next day, I walked into the marbled lobby of 30 Rockefeller Center, where *The David Letterman Show* production team was based, past José Maria Sert's *American Progress* mural with its vast depiction of muscled titans, grim laborers, diaphanous muses and Abe Lincoln in a stovepipe hat, to begin work as a joke writer for a sarcastic guy from Indiana. A uniformed elevator operator glided me to the ninth-floor offices. I was given a window desk that looked across the Avenue of the Americas and somewhat voyeuristically into the photography suite of *Sports Illustrated* magazine, where I'm pretty sure I recognized Martina Navratilova. *Show business has been good to me*, I said to myself. A stack of yellow legal pads and a box of BIC biros sat on the desk, implying I was merely to turn my fertile brain on like a tap and let it flow, baby, let it flow.

At the far end of the room, through an expansive glass cubicle, I could see Letterman and Merrill, the show's head writer. Merrill stood with her fingers laced behind her head. She was studying a chaotically arranged board of colored cards. Letterman stood beside her, a baseball bat resting on his shoulder. Occasionally, he extended the bat to point to one of the cards. Merrill would move the card to another part of the board. Right then, I got the feeling nobody knew what the hell they were doing.

Eventually, Merrill appeared at my desk.

'Welcome,' she said. 'Let's make a TV show. Got any ideas?'

'Millions,' I lied. 'Anything I need to know?'

'Just this: We are at war with the format.'

And that's what we did – made a live show that was completely blind to the sensibilities of what American bumpkins expected when they turned on morning TV. Instead of smarmy game show hosts giving away 'a brand-new car!', viewers were confronted by a gap-toothed Midwesterner showing 'Stupid Pet Tricks' in slow motion or maladroitly interviewing non-celebrities.

One popular recurring segment involved bringing out 'celebrity drop-in Eddie Subitzky', a tall, bespectacled guy who bore an uncanny resemblance to Larry David. A few minutes into each interview, he would throw his hands up and flee the studio. In a comedy club, it was wildly unprofessional. On television, it was subversive.

The show eschewed glitz, extracting its humor from the mundane and the eccentric. One episode was devoted entirely to Sam and Betty Kotinoff, a middle-aged couple celebrating their anniversary. The house band played, a cake was brought out, sparklers were lit, and the studio caught fire on live television because of the pink rose petals soaked in rocket fuel.

To prove the hollow currency of the medium itself, we plucked a random individual from obscurity – Harold Thorkilsen, then CEO of the Ocean Spray Cranberry Corporation – and, through sheer repetition, made him a household name. Every day, we breathlessly lauded his conquests in the cutthroat world of juice-based beverages. Eventually, he contacted the show and asked, 'What is your point?'

There wasn't one, other than to deconstruct every tired trope of what television – and, by extension, America itself – had come to represent. Instead of fusty guests like Steve and Eydie, we dropped watermelons from the sixty-sixth floor of the Rockefeller Center and filmed them exploding on the pavement. I was also given my own segments on the show. I built an entire city out of miniature model train figures called Pitkinville, whose residents were constantly terrorized by household appliances. I made video inserts where I was camping on a traffic island in the middle of Park Avenue or visiting a local concession that sold frozen yoghurt in a shoe.

The show garnered a rabid student following, high-handed reviews from *Newsweek* and *TV Guide* and a hipster distinction. We got mountains of fan mail. I'd walk out on the streets of New York and get recognized. And, just as I'd imagined, those streets gave back endless inspiration.

In September, I moved my notebooks and clothes out of Passaic, New Jersey, and into a perfectly unassuming studio apartment on East 52nd Street. A delivery van showed up with a sleek new sleeper-sofa. I razored the carton from around it and slept atop an island of cardboard. The next day, I went into the office and was informed *The David Letterman Show* had been cancelled. Apparently, for every fan letter the show garnered, there were twenty belligerent ones addressed to the Chairman of NBC from viewers who couldn't understand why the great American largesse of cabin cruisers and Honolulu getaways had been replaced by a dog who could answer a telephone. If Letterman was devastated, he didn't show it. I think he knew his future was cemented, that this was just an aberration.

Three months after the show went off the air, we won an Emmy for 'Best Daytime Variety Show'. No one had invited me to the ceremony, and the Academy shipped my award postage due. I went down to a Lower Manhattan post office branch to collect it. I unwrapped it at the post office, read my name on the brass plate and briefly considered giving an impromptu acceptance speech to the desultory crowd queueing for stamps.

A curious older gentleman in a fat bundled scarf sidled over to inspect it. His face creased with disdain.

'I turned that show on once,' he said. 'I don't even know what I was supposed to be watching.'

'What you were watching,' I replied, 'was night people trying to do a day people's job.'

SNIGLETS

My favorite word in the English language, or any other language for that matter, is 'petrichor'. It's the smell that raindrops make hitting the earth after a long, dry interval. It's also my favorite fragrance – more than orange blossoms, southern breezes, suntan lotion or a new baseball glove. It's the smell of rejuvenation and brings out my inner Proust.

The first time I heard the word, I remember being astonished that it existed. It seemed so specific and euphonic. I began to think about other words that should be in the dictionary but weren't.

Cheedle: the residue left on one's fingers after consuming Cheetos.

Squatcho: the useless button on the top of a baseball cap.

Carperpetuation: the act, when vacuuming, of running over a string or a piece of lint at least a dozen times, reaching over, picking it up, examining it, then putting it back down to give the vacuum *one more chance.*

Eventually, I published five compendiums of those neologisms. I called them 'sniglets', and the books regularly snaked their way up *The New York Times* bestseller list, albeit under the 'Advice, How-to & Miscellaneous' category. Anyone who monetizes success would say they put me in the driver's seat. But look where that gets you. They became a hindrance to my self-perceived sense of artistry, and you could chart my waning enthusiasm by studying the publicity photos of me on the back covers.

In the early eighties, the first book – titled simply *Sniglets* – shot to number two, outsold only by the Rand McNally *Road Atlas* – yes, that old nemesis – and the photo shows a vigorous young carnivore who would relish the chance to meet this Rand McNally fella, punch his lights out and let him know who's *really* going places. By the release of *When Sniglets Ruled the Earth*, the final compendium, I'm glowering insipidly, dangling a Marlboro, slightly out of focus. The rut has clearly set in. None of my comedic achievements eclipsed those books. I couldn't seem to escape them.

I'd first introduced the words as a sketch on the HBO series *Not Necessarily the News*, a remake of the popular UK show *Not the Nine O'Clock News*. It was there I learned the blunt reality of TV writing: you lay the rail but you don't drive the train. Legally, the show's producers *owned the words I'd invented.* They turned the concept into a commercial locomotive, set the dead man's switch and sent it careening. There were *Sniglets* greeting cards. A syndicated *Sniglets* cartoon panel. A *Sniglets* board game. Even (I swear to God), *Sniglets* toilet paper. I fretted over my integrity and cashed the checks. My advice to anyone starting out in television: protect your intellectual property. And the dumb stuff as well.

Still, in stand-up circles, I was killing it in North America. I was a familiar face on all the late-night talk shows, where men – chosen for their white, Midwestern sensibilities – sit behind a desk and introduce you. You walk out to a snappy house band salute, stand on a designated mark and deliver an airtight, six-minute monologue to an audience of out-of-towners, whose bovine attendance can now be checked off their bucket list. Then the host invites you over to sit *in proximity* to his desk. This stratification is made very apparent. You can sit *next* to the desk, but you will never sit *behind* it. Like I cared. The main reason I became a comedian was to avoid desks.

I was headlining all the clubs – tawdry monstrosities with names like Sir Laughs-A-Lot or P. Yopantz. In America, your immortality as an artist exists in the lag between a table of morons laughing at your jokes then ponying up for six piña coladas and a combo-platter of buffalo wings, chili cheese fries and jalapeño poppers. The club owners – coke-addled vipers, by and large – would advertise the show as 'Rich Hall: Creator of Sniglets', knowing that would put asses in seats, even though I'd explicitly told them I didn't do sniglets onstage. Invariably, at some point in the show, someone would yell '*Sniglets!*' and a standoff would ensue. The club owners were enraged by my refusal to indulge. On more than one occasion, they communicated this displeasure via an inarticulate bouncer or one of the club's vaguely gangster-ish 'investors'.

*

In the early fall of 1984, I was booked to do a concert at Auburn University in Alabama. I realize there's a cheap joke in there about the mutual exclusivity of the words 'Alabama' and 'higher learning', but I won't succumb. I grew up in the South and my most irresponsible memories are still there.

The nearest airport to Auburn is in Columbus, Georgia, thirty-five miles to the east. My flight landed about 4.30 in the afternoon. Heading to baggage claim, I noticed that the departure lounges had rocking chairs overlooking both the runway and the flat autumnal haze beyond – a genial down-home touch.

Hertz, National and Avis all gave me the same open-palmed apology: big football homecoming weekend, no cars. I went out to the curbside, found a cab and told the driver I needed to get to Auburn University. He shrugged wordlessly. I threw my suitcase in the back seat and settled in for the journey.

Six minutes later, he pulled up in front of the Columbus bus station.

'What's this?' I asked. 'I need to get to Auburn.'

'I ain't licensed ta drive in the state of Alabama,' he explained. 'You gawn there, they's a dispatcher'll getcha cab over ta Auburn.'

I wanted to ask him why he wasn't allowed to drive in Alabama, but something told me he would take the question contemptuously. So I settled the fare and hauled my suitcase into the station. Inside, the cab dispatcher smiled, called me 'sugar' and told me to take a seat. 'Might be three, four minutes,' she informed me. 'Rush hour, sugah.'

I sat down. The place smelled of chili dogs and Pine-Sol. A few passengers languished on worn wooden benches, looking like they were in no hurry to get anywhere. A small girl stood behind her mother, styling the mom's hair with a brush and a wet paper towel. A hound dog – or possibly a hyena – walked in, pitched up in a patch of afternoon sunlight, looked around, changed its mind and wandered out again. The big clock on the wall read almost five o'clock. Yessiree, rush hour.

A bus from Atlanta arrived, disgorging passengers. In the ensuing bustle, a man took a seat across from me and nodded with just the smallest movement of his head. He wore khaki trousers, great red suspenders and a starched white shirt. I acknowledged him, then looked away, aware that he was still eyeing me. It wasn't unnerving. Southerners often stare at outsiders like they're doing a visual credit check.

Five, ten, fifteen minutes passed. I was getting nervous about the gig, so I went back to the dispatcher.

'Can you call that cab again? I'm running a little late.'

'Your driver's right over there,' she said, pointing to the man who'd been sitting across from me.

I walked back over. 'You the cab driver?'

'You the fella wants to go to Auburn?'

'I am.'

'Best be on our way then.'

Sorghum. Red clay. Passing graveyards holding the bones of Confederate soldiers. My driver never spoke, so I took the opportunity to stare at the back of his head – a part of the anatomy that holds peculiar interest for me. Probably because they're the foreground for the majority of people who watch me onstage, tree stumps obscuring my little clearing in the forest.

This driver's head was unwavering, made me think there was nothing in the scenery he hadn't seen a million times. His neck, red and striated, spilled over his collar in a fleshy skirt. A well-fed neck, I concluded. His haircut was an afterthought, probably nothing more than a number at his local barber's. I noted flecks of premature grey. That's probably enough back-of-the-head reportage for now.

His eyes cut to the rear-view mirror, and he caught me staring at him.

'So whatchall goin' up to Auburn for?' he suddenly asked.

Now and then, I get this wild impulse to lie to complete strangers for no other reason than to hear what comes out of my mouth. It's cathartic, a way of balancing the stilted ritual of too many obligatory conversations with sycophantic fans. On the flight down to Columbus, I'd read an article in the complimentary in-flight magazine about a place called Redstone Arsenal, up in northern Alabama. Redstone is a strategic part of the US Army's Missile Command and a high-security center for experimental rocket research. All kinds of clandestine, eyes-only stuff goes on up there, and I'd found the story fascinating.

I leaned forward and said: 'Well, between you and me, I work in the Ballistic Missile Operations up there at Redstone.' His eyes widened. 'We were launching a prototype rocket from the Standard-3 series. Long story short, it's gone a little rogue.'

'Say what?' The car swerved just a fraction.

'Gone off course and headed toward Auburn. I need to get to the relay module at the School of Aeronautics and reset the coordinates so it bypasses Auburn and heads out over the Atlantic, where we can explode it safely.'

'I'll be damned,' he said and stared at the speedometer.

I sat back in my seat, feeling a satisfying flush of audacity. If nothing else, he might pick up the pace. Directly ahead of us, the sun was setting.

Then he said, 'I thought all you did was them *sniglets*.'

I spluttered. In the mirror, I watched my face go tomato-red. From the shape of my mouth, whatever was about to come out of it was going to begin with the letter *O*, but I had no idea what that might be. It occurred to me that my most prudent response would be to throw open the car door and hurl myself out at seventy miles per hour.

Finally, I said, 'Ohhhhh . . . Well, that's just a little sideline when I'm not working on, you know . . .'

'Them rockets . . .'

'Yeah. I'm also a stand-up comedian. I might do a little show while I'm up there at the school.'

'Y'don't say.'

'In fact, you're welcome to stick around and watch. Then you could drive me back to Columbus.'

He took a moment to answer, as if tugging at his words from the depths of consideration.

'Naw,' he finally said. 'I reckon I better get out of there before that rocket hits.'

CHAPTER 3

SHIPROCK

It is pretty much a showbiz given that when you leave the cast of *Saturday Night Live*, you go directly into a bad film. *Oh! Heavenly Dog, National Lampoon's Animal House, Corky Romano, Joe Dirt, It's Pat, The Ladies Man, Deuce Bigalow: Male Gigolo.* The list goes on and on.

So it was for me, as well. I was a cast member for the 1984–85 season, alongside Billy Crystal, Julia Louis-Dreyfus, Martin Short and Chris Guest. It was a phenomenal year – we pulled the ratings out of the gutter, salvaged the show's dismal reputation and then were all summarily fired.

Soon after, I was summoned to the office of Dino De Laurentiis, producer-grandee of cinema epics. He stood beside his handsome desk and asked if I'd ever seen *It's a Mad, Mad, Mad, Mad World*. The blue carpet on the floor was so thick it practically swallowed his loafers. The furniture was white leather. A huge wall of windows looked out in the direction of the ocean, where an accelerating Phantom fighter jet was leaving an afterburner smudge on a sky the color of the *Hotel California* album. It was November 1986.

Of course, I'd seen *It's a Mad, Mad, Mad, Mad World*. Spencer Tracy, Jonathan Winters, Phil Silvers. A classic.

'I'm going to remake it,' said Dino De Laurentiis, the man who had produced *Serpico*. My Los Angeles agent, the delirious Debbie Miller, pitched forward on the couch and practically genuflected.

'That's an absolutely wonderful idea!' she bleated.

Dino De Laurentiis went over to the window. He was quite old but carried all he'd accomplished in his stride. And why wouldn't he? He'd produced *King Kong*.

'In my version,' he said, 'the cast finds four million dollars. They lose the first three million to various comedic mishaps. Do you know how they lose the final million?'

'How?' asked Debbie, breathless.

'To the audience,' replied the man who had produced *Three Days of the Condor*. 'We are going to give away one million dollars to the first viewer who figures out where the money is hidden in the movie.'

'What a brilliant idea!' Debbie said.

What a horrible idea, I thought and asked him why.

He pointed with a tanned, bony finger at something twenty-three stories below. 'Imagine there's a cinema down there, a twin-plex. People are lining up, wondering which movie to see. One screen is playing *Blue Velvet*, a David Lynch film. Post-production is wrapping as we speak. It features multiple rape scenes and a severed ear . . .'

I started to say, 'I love David Lynch,' but he was obviously going somewhere with this.

'The other film,' he said, 'is giving away a trash bag with a million dollars in it. Young man, which film are people going to choose?'

Anyone with half an ounce of intelligence is going to choose rape and a severed ear over a transparently cynical attempt to propel current cinema to new depths of depravity, I thought. But I said, 'The trash bag film,' because I was talking to the man who had produced *Conan the Barbarian*.

'Yes,' he said. 'And they will come back to see it again and again to search for more clues.' He turned and looked at me. 'I want you in my comedy. You are a very funny man.'

I looked over at Debbie. She was in Fifteen Percent Heaven, already wondering what particular champagne suited this occasion.

'Is there a script?' I asked the man who had produced *Amityville II: The Possession*.

'Somewhat. But it's all edges and no middle.'

'What's that mean?'

'It means the cast is going to improvise huge parts of the film. As in the original.'

'Perfect!' shouted Debbie, who had only yesterday booked me as a guest for an event called The Micky Dolenz Celebrity Invitational Ski Tournament.

'I'll need to think about it,' I said.

I went home and promptly forgot about it.

The following day Debbie called with the offer: fourteen weeks of shooting in Arizona, December through February, mostly around

Glen Canyon. Glen Canyon is fucking freezing in the winter. I explicitly told her I didn't want to do it. She told me the fee. I explicitly told her I wanted to do it.

There was the usual back and forth. When it was all worked out, the man who had brought Fellini's *La Strada* to the screen stuck me in one of the most abysmal productions in the history of cinema.

The entire cast and crew were sequestered at the Lake Powell Resort Lodge in Page, Arizona, near the north rim of Glen Canyon, which was desolately beautiful with gorgeous, striated cliffs and shimmering bristlecone pines. Snow dusted the mesas. Golden eagles soared above in the Delft blue sky. Our director turned up senile.

We were summoned to the lodge's function room for a meet-and-greet. Kevin Pollak, later to win accolades in *A Few Good Men* and *The Usual Suspects*, was there, as was Eddie Deezen from *Grease*, whose specialty was playing nerds. The veteran character actor Royce Applegate was asleep. At the end of the front row, Tom Bosley, the father from the sitcom *Happy Days*, was popping breath mints and emanating nascent enthusiasm – particularly toward Penny Baker, *Playboy*'s fortieth anniversary centerfold, cast no doubt for her acute thespian talents. An associate producer named Coomby, who looked like an angry surfer, stepped forward and introduced himself.

'I'm told we're missing a cast member, but I'll start anyway.' He handed out a stack of papers. 'NDAs. Non-Disclosure Agreements. Sign in indelible ink. Discussion of any aspect of this film to anyone outside cast and crew is grounds for dismissal. I don't care if it's Grandma on her deathbed. Get this straight: *you are not eligible to win the million dollars.* Maybe you're thinking, "I'll go through a third party. I know a few coke dealers. That is to say, I know them, but I don't know them. Wink, wink. Nudge, nudge." Think again. Dino De Laurentiis is too shrewd for that. He made Arnold Schwarzenegger a global phenomenon. Another thing: if you're thinking of ransacking the locations for the money, forget it. I would assume most of you – but not all of you – know it's only *figuratively* hidden. There will be all kinds of vital clues buried in this film, as well as red herrings and verbal misdirection. Do not question their significance. Mind your own business and let us do our job. Your job is to make a funny film. Have fun, chums.'

Coomby then ceded the room to a brands representative from The Glad Products Company. Plain suit. Dull shoes. No one caught the guy's name. He held his hands together as if addressing a convocation.

'Glad Bags,' he said, 'is excited to be part of this project, our first foray into cinema—'

Suddenly Rick Overton, my friend and the heretofore missing cast member, flung himself through the doorway. He was a big, dramatic-looking fellow, inexplicably dressed for the meeting in a one-piece snowmobile suit. The upper half was undone and draping from his waist. He looked like he was emerging from a cocoon.

The brands rep pretended to ignore him. 'Our products will be featured throughout the film, reminding viewers Glad is the nation's leader in trashcan liners, lawn and garden bags, zip-lock sandwich bags—'

'And drug paraphernalia!' Rick bayed with alarming verve. He reeled past us, studying our faces like the line-up of a sports team.

'Every ounce of weed I ever bought in my life came in a Glad sandwich bag. Wish I'd bought stock in it twenty years ago.' He turned to the rep. 'Who, by the way, are you?'

'I represent Glad.'

'And why should we give a shit?' He turned back to us. 'We're here to make a comedy, not peddle trash bags. Am I right?'

We all half-mumbled in agreement.

'Who's seen *It's a Mad, Mad, Mad, Mad World*. Anyone?'

Some of us nodded.

'One of the all-time greats, Phil Silvers!' Rick proceeded to launch into a Sergeant Bilko impression that was spot on – and an obvious attempt to assert himself as the cast alpha.

Now awake, Royce Applegate said, 'Relax, Overton. You already got the part.'

The rep, trying to win back the proceedings, continued. 'As I was saying—'

'You've said it, bagboy. We get it,' Rick said. 'Here's a little blabbing motion I make with my hands to indicate you talk too much.' He made the blabbing motion with his hands.

The meeting quickly disassembled, and we set out to make a bad, bad, bad, bad movie.

As the days progressed, a kind of anarchy befell the cast. No one had the slightest idea what we were doing, and our attempts at improvisation generally devolved into jockeying for camera close-ups. At this, Rick Overton was the master manipulator. He somehow ended up front and center in every scene.

I'd known Rick since our days starting out in New York, and he was a formidable improviser, the only person I'd ever seen who could go toe-to-toe onstage with Robin Williams. It was apparent he meant to use this film to showcase his range. But he was all over the place. His accents and mannerisms shifted day to day, leaving the rest of us baffled. For instance, he chose to play one entire scene as Sean Connery. This had a reciprocal effect on Kevin Pollak, who chose to play his character as Peter Falk's Columbo. Our director, Richard Fleischer, ambled off the set and retired to his trailer for a nap.

My role was a deranged Vietnam vet named Slaughter – a character that had served me well earlier in my career. My first few scenes were opposite Penny Baker, cast assiduously against type as a stripper. Between takes, she revealed that she'd been an actress her entire life, although further questioning revealed that she had *not* been an actress for maybe twenty-two of those twenty-three years, and the year she *was* an actress may have only been for several weeks at the age of six. I was willing to accept this discrepancy because, well, she was a Playmate.

Richard Fleischer's directorial approach, when he wasn't napping, consisted of stuffing his hands in his coat pocket, leaning forward with authority and croaking, 'Roll,' in a sad, hoarse whisper. When he'd seen enough, rather than yell, 'Cut,' he would divulge something vaguely personal about himself. Thus, we learned: (a) thank God, this was his last film; (b) it was both facilitator and impediment to him purchasing a twenty-four-foot Boston Whaler and sailing to the Dry Tortugas; and (c) the 'blonde with the rack' couldn't act 'for nickels' but was still the only damn thing worth watching in this 'shit-show'.

In the daily 'woodshedding' meetings, which the entire cast was required to attend, I attempted to write myself out of the movie. There was a scene where Slaughter was required to accidentally drop a trash bag full of a million dollars off a cliff.

'The bag gets stuck on a ledge,' I proffered. 'I climb down to retrieve it, slip, and end up hanging on to an icicle for dear life. The whole cast is breathless, waiting for me to recover the money. Someone says, "You know what they say about the weather around here. Wait five minutes and it'll change." Cut to the sun coming out from a cloud. Cut back to the cast. They're all in shirtsleeves, sweating. Snap. Sound of me screaming. Someone shrugs and says, "Let's hit the pool".'

Richard Fleischer looked around the table in bafflement, then at me. 'Let me get this straight, you die?'

'Well, yeah.'

'Someplace else you'd rather be?' asked Coomby, seeing right through this ruse.

One night, I woke to the roar of a snowmobile under my window and intense white light splashing across the motel walls. A minute later, I heard Rick storm into his room, right next to mine. He sounded like a mastodon. The walls were thin plaster and I lay there, listening to him teaching himself Spanish through headphones. Every time I nodded off, something demented like 'Tengo un lapiz amarillo!' would jolt me back awake. This went on until 2am. Then he stomped about imitating a baritone radio announcer: 'Sunday, Sunday, Sunday! It's monster funny-car, quarter-mile mayhem as

"Big Daddy" Don Garlits and Tommy "Instant" Ivo chase three-time world-elimination champion Shirley "Cha-Cha" Muldowney at the Daytona Motor Speedway. Action, action, Sunday! Be there!' Something told me this new character would be making an appearance on camera soon.

I pounded on the wall.

'I hear ya,' he yelled back.

I nodded off again only to lurch awake to the sound of Rick yelling 'Sweet honey in the rock!' repeatedly. I heard a chair clatter furiously across his floor. Then he was banging on my door.

'What is it, Rick?'

'Open up, man.'

'It's three-thirty . . .'

'Open up, man. I gotta talk to you.'

I let him in. He was in his snowmobile suit and reeked of diesel. He put a finger to his lips telling *me* to pipe down. 'I know where the money's hidden!'

'Where?'

He pushed past me, turned on a bedside light and whipped the curtains closed. 'Shiprock, New Mexico.'

'*Where?*'

'Remember the police station scene? The old sheriff's name was Chip Monk Sr. It was on his desk plate.' He opened his script, full of scribblings. 'It's an anagram for Shiprock, NM. So is the name above the hardware store, next to the chili stand where Tom has the heart attack: Morphnicks. I always knew dyslexia would pay off one day.'

I looked at the names. 'So what? We're ineligible for the money,

Rick.' Still, there was the feeling of something conspiratorial passing between us.

'There's nothing to stop us from looking for it though, is there?'

'I signed an NDA.'

'I didn't. Well, I *did*, but as Phil Silvers.' He pulled a phone directory from my bedside table and thumbed to a regional map, pointing vaguely to the area near the Four Corners, where Arizona, Utah, Colorado and New Mexico meet. 'Somewhere up in here. I reckon a three-hour drive.'

'Why are you telling me?'

'My license is revoked. Six points for speeding.'

'You want me to drive you to some godforsaken part of New Mexico? What would we be looking for?'

'Specificity. A cabin, a cave, a marker, coordinates . . . I don't know exactly, but there'll be something there that ties it to the money. I can feel it.'

His eyes were wide as silver dollars, and he appeared to be breathing through his teeth. I felt like I was trapped in a hot car with an anxious dog. 'And what happens when we find it?'

'We leak the location.'

'To whom?'

'*Everyone.* Flood the pipeline. Spread the word. Call the *National Enquirer*, some shit. All I'm saying is, if everyone knows where the money's hidden, Glad Bags is fucked. They'll ditch the whole stupid gimmick. Then, instead of a bunch of yahoos coming to our movie 'cause they think they're on a fucking treasure hunt, we've got people coming to see real entertainment.'

'I'm not sure I'd call it entertainment.'

'What would you call it?' He looked genuinely bewildered.

'I think we're turkey stuffing, Rick. And I've got no one to blame but myself. I shoulda turned this movie down.'

He shook his head. 'You are so wrong, man. We've shot a lot of quality stuff – funny stuff. I know it's all over the place, but so was *Mad, Mad World*. Look how that turned out.'

'They had Spencer Tracy. We have . . . you.'

He dropped the directory on the bed. 'Let me tell you something about movie-making because you seem a little naïve: it's all about purity.'

'Purity?'

'All that money, investment, equipment, production. Hundreds of people running around like an ant colony. Tension. Nerves. Expectation. And it all funnels down through a single aperture. Somebody says, 'Roll,' and *we* have to nail it. That's the purity of the moment, man.'

'Are we in the same movie?'

'And you wanna let some trash bag assholes come along and ruin that for us? No fucking way, man. We can *purify* this thing.'

This is probably a good time to mention that Rick was a recovering alcoholic/coke fiend, who had the addict's attribute of throwing himself into every pursuit with overarching zeal. Previous fixations included Harley-Davidsons, mega-vitamins, Thai kickboxing, the books of William Gibson, world-domination conspiracies, amateur hypnotism, and now – judging from his presiding attire – snowmobiling. It was hard not to get swept along by such manic fervor. The guy was my friend.

'I don't know, Rick,' I said.

'C'mon man, I'm going stir-crazy on this fucking set. Action, action, *goddamn* I want some action.'

'Alright, I'll think about it. Get out of here.'

He left. I climbed back into bed and drifted off to sleep, in awe of the delusions that kept him going.

The following evening, I got a lift from one of the transport coordinators to the public library in Page. I wanted to read up on Shiprock. I wasn't ready to accept Rick's idea as an actuality, but I admit I *was* intrigued. Turned out, Rick was there too. At a big empty table, making random, frenetic notes all over the pages of his script.

'You following me?' he asked. His face was wind-burnished, hair askew.

'Just doing a little research,' I said.

He shoved a large book in my direction: *New Mexico: Portraits of a Land and its People.*

'This is what you're looking for.' He pointed to a section on Shiprock. It was a giant rock hill located on Navajo tribal land and named Shiprock because, viewed from a distance, it resembled a vast clipper ship sailing on an empty sea. The geologic term for the landform was *monadnock*, a lone-standing mountain. Also, I realized, a word tantalizingly close to Penny Baker's stripper alias in the film: Mona D. Nockers.

I looked up to see Rick grinning at me from his private universe.

'We're gonna need a four-wheel drive,' he said.

*

Later, when we both had a two-day break in shooting, I rented a red Jeep Cherokee – transfer case, ten-ply snow tires, the whole deal. Sneaking off the set was a contract violation. But then, I supposed, so was scuttling a mega-million-dollar film campaign.

When Rick climbed into the passenger seat, he looked at me hard and said, 'This is the last time we use our real names. Anyone around that mountain asks what we're doing, we tell them we're arrowhead hunters. Make an impression on no one.'

I had to laugh. It was impossible for Rick Overton not to make an impression.

We drove east on Highway 64 into emptiness. Red rock and scrubby rangeland, the occasional elk wandering out onto the highway. It's always thrilled me to see wild animals doing something besides staring at you dead-eyed from above a fireplace, and I slowed down a few times to marvel. Rick seemed impatient. He was trawling through his script and kept looking up to check the speedometer.

'Pick up the slack will ya?' he said. 'Drive it like you stole it.'

'Take it easy, Rick. This road is crawling with critters.'

He gawked around with irritation, then sought something listenable on the radio. All we got was a thin, Hispanic-language broadcast from Albuquerque: Mexican Easy Listening. This gave him a chance to practice his horrendous Spanish. 'La musica! La musica! Esta la esa Neil Diamond.'

That went on for half an hour. I thought, *I could dump his body out here and no one would find it for weeks.*

Near the Teec Nos Pos trading post, a light tail-wheel aircraft overtook us from above. We watched it land on the highway, cruise for a few hundred yards and go aloft again. This time, it banked sharply to the left and glided low over a vast cattle range. A herd of desultory cows looked up to see hay bales dropping out of the sky.

'Miras! Miras! Las vacas!' Rick shouted moronically.

That was enough. I killed the radio.

Crossing the New Mexico state line, we hit a snow squall. I had to shift to four-wheel drive and creep along at twenty. I could feel the agitation coming off Rick.

'Rick, what makes you think we're even going to be allowed on tribal land?'

'Just play it cool. *Arrowheads*, remember? Damn. I could've gotten here faster by snowmobile.'

'Look around,' I said. 'It's desolation. *Who* would even picture stashing a million dollars out here? None of this adds up.'

The storm cleared as quickly as it had started, and Shiprock suddenly loomed before us, a hulking ghostship against an orange sky. It looked like a mountain auditioning to be in a movie. Right away, it *all* made sense.

Rick made a low whistle. 'It's like the Devils Tower,' he said. 'From *Close Encounters*.'

He was right. Maybe it was the way the lowering sun bathed Shiprock in radiance, but it felt like we were being compelled toward it. Not mystically, as in *Close Encounters* – more financially. It occurred to me that *Close Encounters* would have been a whole different film if the aliens had emerged from the UFO carrying a trash bag full of a million dollars.

We drove for another twenty minutes, the mountain slowly engulfing us in its magnitude, until we reached an unpaved road that appeared to lead straight up to its base, bordered on one side by a sheer natural dike. Daylight was waning. The snow had turned the path to gumbo. I gripped the steering wheel hard to keep the thing on the road. We slogged along over ruts and boulders. Rick gaped out the window. There was nothing – just snow whipping around in the gullies.

'We've got no business out here,' I said.

'Let's just see what's around the bend.'

'There's no bend, Rick.'

Trying to turn around, I slid the back end of the Jeep into a ditch. I tried the old rocking-free maneuver, but the rear wheels just spun. Rick cursed and wrenched open his door. He trudged around to the back of the Jeep and got a shoulder up against it. It took about ten minutes of gruntwork before the tires finally spun clear. Then, as he was heading back to the passenger side, I had a moment of absolute and ultimate clarity. *Why flood the pipeline*, I realized, *when it was possible, just possible, to shut down the entire waterworks?* I reached over, grabbed Rick's script, eased my door open ever-so-slightly, and tossed it underneath the car.

Rick climbed back in, out of breath, splattered in mud and snow.

'We get a motel,' he said. 'Get something to eat, back here tomorrow morning.'

'I've seen enough, Rick. Let's get back to Page.'

'No chance, Kemo Sabe. Remind me to buy some disposable cameras. We document everything, right?'

I didn't answer. I was watching two uneven cones of headlights bouncing up the road toward us. As they got closer, I could make out the dark mass of a sedan. Alarmingly, Rick jumped out and walked in front of its path, waving his arms. *What the fuck?* I thought.

The sedan, an old lurching Chevrolet, stopped. After what seemed an extraordinarily long time, both front doors opened simultaneously. The two men who emerged appeared to be Navajo. There was an odd patience in the way they approached Rick. One of them, a burly fellow in a worn military coat and a baseball cap, did all the talking. The other one hung back, occasionally throwing glances in my direction. I watched Rick's animated gestures and wondered what the hell he was talking to them about. After a few minutes, he returned.

'What was that?' I said.

'I asked if there were any motels nearby. He said keep going another five miles up this road. We'd have our choice of a Marriott or a Hilton. Funny guy.'

'Good thing you didn't make much of an impression.'

'He said the mountain is a consecrated animal slain by his ancestors. But if we bought them a tankful of gas, the spirits might be willing to look the other way.'

'There's no gas out here, Rick.'

'He said to go to the Amoco in Farmington and leave twenty bucks with the clerk behind the counter. I guess that amounts to permission.'

We watched the old Chevy turn around and head back down the road. I waited for it to create some distance, then started up the

Jeep and pulled away. In the rear-view mirror, I could just make out Rick's script lying in the snow, the wind riffling its pages like invisible fingers.

We got motel rooms in Farmington, New Mexico, a town that looked like it had packed up in the middle of the night and left. Windowless storehouses, pyramids of fuel barrels, abandoned vehicles. The motel had an adjoining bar, and we went in for burgers. It was pretty much a Native clientele. Rick kept staring rudely like a freshman anthropologist. He also had a habit of constantly picking up his napkin between thumb and forefinger and shaking out the crumbs. A waitress came over and set a new one down in front of him.

'If you're worried about smallpox,' she said, 'we managed to eradicate it about a hundred years ago.' Rick grinned at her vacantly.

A couple of Navajo girls approached our table. 'You the guys that bought Dallas the tank of gas?'

'Yeah,' I answered. Word must have gotten around.

'What were you doing up on the Shiprock?' the older, taller girl asked. She was dressed like a cowgirl in jeans and a snap-button shirt. A ristra of green, plastic chili peppers adorned her neck.

'Looking for arrowheads,' Rick said hastily.

A moment of silence. Then the other girl said, 'As a rule, they're much easier to find when the sun's still up. Why don't you buy the two of us a beer?'

'I don't drink,' said Rick.

'We do.'

I went to the bar and ordered three Coors. It is a truth universally acknowledged that two Navajo girls letting a white man buy them beers must be in possession of boyfriends. Sure enough, while I was collecting the beers, they walked in and pulled up chairs on either side of Rick. I recognized one of them as the guy who had asked us to buy him gas – Dallas, I presumed. I had a sense of the room closing in on us and thought we should probably leave. But, by the time I got back to the table, Rick was practically conducting a seminar on arrowheads to a thoroughly disinterested party of four: '. . . in particular your Plano clusters, which are very prevalent in this part of New Mexico. They have a more concave base than, say, your Escobas or Soto-points.'

Like I said, he was a hell of an improviser.

Dallas waved a large hand as if to say, 'Enough already.' He watched me set the beers down on the table. I started to slide two across to the girls.

'We ordered orange juice,' the older girl said abruptly. There was the slightest flicker in her eye that conveyed *don't*.

'You did indeed,' I replied. 'They're on the way.'

Dallas's eyes bored into mine. 'You order three beers for yourself?' he said.

'I certainly did. I have a drinking problem!'

I sought to alleviate the tension by asking if anyone was hungry. They all were. I ordered four hamburger platters that, along with numerous pints of orange juice and the full tank of gas, pretty much followed a long historical line of placation of indigenous people by whites. In this way, Rick and I were able to cement their approval to hunt on the Shiprock for arrowheads – which, of course, was not our true intention, also in line with history.

By the time I'd downed the third beer, whatever cordial suspicion we'd raised seemed to have disappeared. From what I could gather, the two girls – Juanita and Nachsa – were cousins, Dallas and Juanita were a couple, and the guy with Dallas was cousin to one of the girls but, confusingly, not the other. He never spoke the entire time we sat there, and Dallas said his name was Mike Sits-and-Stares. I thought that might be a joke, but I didn't ask.

Rick maintained his low profile throughout the evening by regaling our table guests – and eventually the entire bar – with a note-perfect recreation of Robert Shaw's USS Indianapolis speech from *Jaws*. Afterward, he attempted to hypnotize Mike Sits-and-Stares, using Juanita's pepper necklace as a pendulum. Mike Sits-and-Stares proved stoically resistant to the idea. It began to feel like we were wearing out our welcome, so we made our excuses and headed back to the motel.

Rick said he'd wake me up first thing in the morning. Ten minutes later, he was knocking on my door.

'Where's the car keys?' he said. 'I think I left my script in the Jeep.'

Around nine, the following morning, my phone rang. The Bureau of Indian Affairs wished to speak with us.

I let Rick do all the talking.

'Explain this,' said the BIA Special Agent. He was fortyish, weathered-looking and had the restless posture of someone who didn't like being indoors. A black Stetson rested on his desk. He lifted it to reveal Rick's script.

'It's a film script,' Rick said.

'I know it's a film script. Yours?'

'Yessir.'

'How did it end up on Shiprock?'

'It must've fallen out of the car.'

The agent picked it up. 'From what I can tell, it's a bunch of crazy people running around with bags of money.'

'Glad Trash Bags, to be exact,' Rick said, clearly looking to transfer some blame.

'And you two are part of this foolishness?'

'Right.'

'You're movie stars?'

'Well, I wouldn't . . .'

The agent found a page on which Rick had scrawled *Shiprock* in pen. Underlined. Circled. 'Your handwriting?'

'Yessir.'

'Not *sir*. You get to call me *Chief*.' Chief dropped the script back onto his desk and shot a finger toward the window. 'Is there money hidden on that mountain out there?'

'Only figuratively.'

'*Figuratively* . . .' Chief chewed on that word for a moment. 'That the same as *imaginary*?'

'It is. Chief, look, we don't mean to cause any—'

Chief raised a hand for silence. 'An elder, out walking his dog, found your script this morning. He took it home and showed it to his kids. They didn't know what to make of it. They called me.' He leaned back and touched his fingertips together. 'The Navajo – or Diné, as we call ourselves – have a very strong oral tradition. We don't write things down, we pass them along by word. And every time those words get passed along, they get embellished a little more. Which explains how that big, dead volcanic plug sitting out there *transmogrified* into a great, winged bird-monster that carried our ancestors to this very special place. You like that word: *transmogrified*?'

'Good word, Chief.'

'Hell of a word. With that in mind, how long do you think it will take before your *figurative* money *transmogrifies* into *real* money, and I've got half the population of our sovereign little nation crawling around that rock looking for it? Well, I'll tell you: probably *already*.' He stood up, came around his desk and loomed over us. 'Somebody's going to fall into a crevice. Somebody's going to break their neck. I'm going to have to station a half-dozen of my agents out there to turn folks back, explain to them it's a hoax perpetrated by a couple of idiots. And you *couple of idiots* are going back to your Powers That Be to inform them that if the mountain so much as gets *mentioned* in their little film, they're going to feel the full might of the BIA *and* the Navajo Nation. And that's a considerable might. We clear?'

'You got it, Chief,' Rick said.

'Mind if I hold on to this script?'

'Be my guest.'

'Thanks. Get off the rez.'

As we pulled out of the BIA parking lot, Rick remarked, 'Tell you something about the Navajo, that is one sarcastic nation. Where do you reckon they get it from?'

I turned left, heading back on 64 West toward Page. Rick promptly closed his eyes to get a few winks. I couldn't believe how unfazed he seemed by the encounter. Me? I was about to jump out of my skin.

I drove a few hundred yards to the Highway 491 intersection and sat at the stop sign, looking around, waiting for the trucks to pass. There were a few shabby houses about, their roofs bristling with antennas, windowsills full of figurines. Diagonally across the four-way, a lone Navajo, smoking a cigarette, hunkered in front of a gaily painted Hatch chili pepper stand. The stand was boarded up for the winter, but the perspective was dazzling: a forlorn figure contrasted against vibrant red and green. Beyond that, the great mountain Shiprock, in full frame, filled the distance. It was a cinematic view.

What really caught my eye, though, was the sign above the stand: CHILIES BY THE BULK. On either side of the words, someone had painted a pair of large trash bags, black with green chilies cascading over the sides.

I thought back to the scene we'd shot where Tom Bosley's character has a heart attack from eating hot peppers. Hatch chilies are renowned for their fieriness.

The day and the road and the sky were now *all* crystal clear, and I drove back toward Arizona feeling like a million bucks. Well, *figuratively* anyway.

The BIA agent had been right about the power of oral tradition. Within two days, it seemed like every member of the Navajo Nation knew the money was hidden somewhere around Shiprock. They began to drift in and sometimes *onto* the set, searching everywhere for specific clues. They badgered the crew, continuously interrupted takes and made numerous ill-timed enquiries as to when – *exactly* when – they could officially enter the sweepstakes.

Filming shut down. The following day, Coomby gathered us all together in the function room. He picked at a bit of lint on his shirt-sleeve, lifted his eyes to engage mine and never took them off me as he announced that due to 'circumstances unforeseen', the production would be relocating to Lake Havasu City, Arizona.

It all backfired. We ended up reshooting every scene that alluded to Shiprock. No one was allowed to go home for Christmas. Shooting ran over by two weeks, for which we were paid the minimum contractual overtime fee.

When *Million Dollar Mystery* came out in July, roughly 300 viewers guessed correctly that the money was hidden in the Statue of Liberty's nose. A random draw was held, and the million-dollar prize went to a fourteen-year-old girl from Bakersfield, California. The movie itself grossed less than that. Presumably, director Richard Fleischer still made it to the Dry Tortugas.

On the day of the movie's nationwide release, a crew from *Entertainment Tonight* sent Rick and me down to the Egyptian Theatre on Hollywood Boulevard. We were instructed to stand outside and ask viewers emerging from the cinema where they supposed the money was hidden.

We waited. Two couples straggled out and refused to make eye contact. We waited some more – forever it seemed. Finally, a lone, middle-aged man strutted out.

He spotted us, walked up to the camera and, without prompting, said, 'That movie was so bad, I want *everybody's* money back.'

CHAPTER 4

AN HOUR

July 1995. At a Montreal dump called Jimbo's, I was running my six minutes for the upcoming gala at the Just for Laughs international comedy festival. Four minutes in, at the cusp of a critical punchline, someone in the crowd yelled, '*Sniglets!*'

'I don't do *sniglets* onstage,' I said and tried to get back on track.

A few seconds later: 'C'mon! Let's hear some *sniglets*!'

A slow clap spread through the room: '*Snig-lets, snig-lets!*'

'Sniglets are a print fixture,' I explained, for the eighteen-thousandth time in my life. 'They don't transfer to stage any more than Gary Larson can describe a *Far Side* cartoon.' This was met by bafflement and deflation. I might as well have been admonishing a child. I ploughed through the remainder of my set, but the momentum was dead.

The following night at the Just for Laughs gala performance, I stormed it. Same set as Jimbo's, but a more discerning crowd. Afterward, in the schmooze-infested bar of the Delta Hotel, I sat on the edge of a fake wishing well, shooting the breeze with some Canadian comics. The well was a crass promotional feature supplied by the good people of Molson, and I *was*, in fact, drinking a Molson, so . . . mission accomplished.

The comics drifted off, and a woman approached me. In human history, the most mystifying appearance is that of the stranger at the well.

'Night and day, huh?' she said. She was Austrian. She wore her hair in a sleek, expensive-looking bob, offset somewhat by ill-fitting spectacles, which seemed not to want to stay on her face.

'What's that?' I said.

'I watched your set at Jimbo's last night, and I watched it again tonight.'

'Oh, yeah. Night and day.'

'What are *sniglets*, by the way?'

'A disagreeable side effect of my career.'

'My name is Marlene.' She shook my hand fervently, like she was pumping for oil. 'I produce shows for the Edinburgh Fringe.'

'Does Edinburgh pay?' I asked.

She pushed her glasses up on her face. 'Wrong question. Ask me, "Marlene, how can I breathe life back into my moribund career? Where can I go to reclaim my mojo?" Because, frankly, there's a thin line between a groove and a rut.'

'Ouch!' I replied.

'I can say things like that because I'm jet-lagged,' she said. 'And because I don't give a drizzling shit about "development deals" and cable specials, or how many *Tonight Show*s you've done.' She handed me a card. 'You *need* a fluid hour. Something that builds to a satisfying finish. And you need to put it together fast. Think about it.'

On the train from London to Scotland, I brought along a pair of Edinburgh-based novels: *The Prime of Miss Jean Brodie* and *Trainspotting*. Whenever I'm bound for someplace new and exciting, I feel the need to have a visceral grounding, a fixed expectation, preferably from a reliable literary source. From such a perspective, misconceptions turn to revelations. It's travel advice I don't recommend to anyone.

Thirty pages into *The Prime of Miss Jean Brodie*, I had a picture of Edinburgh as a glowering pit of Calvinism, dank and formidable, with the occasional 'burst of epiphanic light falling gracefully onto its grimy streets'. A little heavy-handed, to be honest. I switched over to *Trainspotting* but, five pages in, returned to Miss Brodie's Edinburgh, seeing it as the more pleasant option. I wanted to read more about this *epiphanic light.* It sounded like something I could use a dose of.

Marlene met me at Waverley Station. She was wearing Doc Martens and a buffalo plaid shirt. A leather satchel draped across her torso like an old saddle. She barely uttered a hello before asking, 'How's your hour?'

'I haven't really put it together. I'm working without a net.'

She stared at me grimly. Apparently, no one shows up at the Fringe without an hour.

She brusquely informed me that we had an interview at Radio

Forth, and we headed over the North Bridge past the astonishing Scott Monument, which momentarily stopped me in my tracks. It looked like some kind of baroque rocket ship. We reached the New Town. The streets were coarse and uneven, and clearly had never anticipated wheel-along suitcases such as the one I was currently dragging, making a racket like wet gravel being poured into a wheelbarrow.

Somewhere near Princes Street, we passed an opening in the side of a building that looked like it had been blown out by a mortar shell. The sign above it read 'Big Value Comedy Show'. I poked my head inside and saw a rat eating a donut.

'Marlene, is this an actual venue?'

'Mmmmmmhmmm.'

'This looks like a place where people would come to see comedy if it were illegal.'

'Put a wiggle on it,' she said, and I followed along, an old remora trailing a shark.

In a small cheery guest room at the Radio Forth studio, I waited to be interviewed. Marlene absently thumbed through a Fringe Festival program, tapping her foot impatiently. Each time she jabbed her glasses back against the bridge of her nose, it gave her a new idea.

'You should keep a daily journal while you're here,' she said.

'A journal of what?' I was planning on spending my time creating new jokes.

'Thoughts, sensations, motifs: an American comedian's perspective on the insanity of a month in Edinburgh.'

'Insanity, you say . . .'

'I'll call the editor of the *Edinburgh Evening News*. Maybe they'll run it. You can't buy that kind of publicity.'

'I don't know, Marlene. I think I'd rather just thumb things in slowly. Get the lie of the land first, if you know what I mean.' It must have appeared to her that I was not taking this seriously enough.

'Let me condense things for you: *Hit the ground running*.' She thrust the Fringe program toward me. 'Have you seen what you're up against?'

The foreword to the program breathlessly trumpeted the 'world's largest celebration of creativity, culture and artistic freedom!' There must have been 2,000 shows listed – comedy, dance, theater, art exhibits, music, children's productions, film, lectures, pageants, walking tours. I found a small quarter-page ad with my picture on it and marveled at my profound insignificance in this cultural landscape.

'How the hell does anyone sell any tickets?' I asked. 'There's too much of everything.'

'Word of mouth mainly. If you're funny, news travels fast. So far you've sold a grand total of seventy.'

'Fine by me. I'm not in this for the money, am I?'

'Well, I am.'

'Naturally.' I turned to the middle of the program. A double-page spread showed a silver bottle glimmering in effulgent light. 'What's the Perrier Award?' I asked.

'For best comedian.'

'It's a spray-painted bottle.'

'That spray-painted bottle can make someone's career.'

'I already have a career.' I studied the ridiculous thing for a moment and gave the program back to her. It struck me as crass that a festival claiming to celebrate artistic freedom would let itself be co-opted by a liter of dubious French groundwater. 'You ask me, awards ruin stand-up. We're competitive enough as it is.' A second later: 'Am I eligible?'

'You would be if you actually had a show.'

I winced. She was really driving it home.

The Mark Findlay Show – a kind of current affairs format – was broadcasting live, and someone had thoughtfully placed exterior speakers in the guest room. At this very moment, an irate caller was airing his somewhat unorthodox views on 'Belarus's War'. I was intrigued, both by his accelerated, impenetrable brogue, and because I wasn't aware that Belarus was at war.

'Fandans and fleggers, the lot of them. It hurts mae ears,' he said, or something thrilling to that effect. It enriches one's life to travel to distant places and try to understand what people are saying. The caller seemed to have only a marginal claim on sanity, and when his ultimate summation of the situation was that it was 'all a load o' mince ta sell some crap records', I turned to Marlene.

'Did *you* know Belarus was at war?'

She looked up and listened for a moment.

'Blur/Oasis,' she said. 'He's talking about Blur and Oasis.' She went back to perusing the program.

The next call was a real humdinger. A mother in a breathless, quivering voice described an incident from the previous evening. She had accompanied her eight-year-old son to see a show called Tokyo Shock Boys, under the impression it was to be a solid hour of good old-fashioned gross-out humor. Scorpion-swallowing, screwdrivers up the nasal cavity, that sort of thing. It was the boy's birthday, he'd been anticipating this for months, they'd secured front-row seats. So far, so good. But, apparently at some point, the arena lights had dimmed, and a reclining geisha was wheeled out on a gurney. By the mother's account, the geisha seductively unwrapped her kimono, bifurcated her legs and – as Nine Inch Nails' 'Closer' throbbed from the speakers – a giant Madagascar hissing cockroach emerged from her vagina. The mother's initial and rather vivid assessment of the creature was that it 'resembled a varnished croissant'. The Gallic precision with which she pronounced '*croissant*' seemed – to me – to belie her Scottish accent and a bell of recognition went off in my head. Something was up, and I had a good inkling of what it was. She went on to describe how the cockroach had hurled itself onto the floor, scuttled across the stage and disappeared up her eight-year-old's trouser leg. Now the youngster was traumatized and, according to the mother, suffering both sleepless nights *and* recurring nightmares, which struck me as a unique, if contradictory, nocturnal affliction.

The call finished, and I was ushered into the studio. I took a seat across from Mark Findlay and slipped on a pair of headphones dangling from the side of the desk. The booth was cozy, awash in a warm, whorehouse glow, which I quickly realized was from the flashing red lights of angry callers.

'The American comedian Rich Hall is with us,' Mark said. 'But we need to take a few phone calls first.' This he announced in a casual, mellifluous voice. In fact, he looked wild-eyed and helpless, like an air traffic controller trying to avert a mid-air collision.

The cockroach story had clearly induced civic outrage. I sat there and listened to Mark fend off one tirade after another, a cavalcade of Calvinist indignation. His hands pressed against his headphones like he was absorbing voltage from every call. For me, it was an impromptu language lesson. One caller was *scunnered*. Someone else described the incident as *pure stoter*. A pastor came on, claiming that God's wrath was *thermal*. Who the hell knows what that meant? Several callers demanded the Tokyo Shock Boys be run out of town. I felt bad for Mark, who was merely a filter for all this abuse.

It was twenty minutes before he acknowledged me on air.

'Welcome to Edinburgh, Rich Hall,' he said. 'What do you make of all this, of the Shock Boys' show and the cockroach?'

'I don't think it happened,' I answered.

'No?'

'Publicity stunt. Anyway, Madagascar hissing cockroaches are harmless.'

'You don't say.'

'In some parts of the world, they're used as pets.'

That's all it took. By expressing my doubts, I was somehow seen to be condoning this filth. Caller after caller queued up to level their disgust with me. I was fascinated by how quickly you could piss off a nation's people. Someone referred to me as a *clatty yank bampot*. I had no defense for that. It's hard to counter an epithet if you have to ask for its translation first.

'It doesn't take you long to ingratiate yourself to the community,'

Marlene said afterward. She was walking hurriedly ahead of me as if she wanted to get away. She was *supposed* to be leading me to my flat.

'Why are you so angry? It's just a radio show.'

She stopped and turned. 'That station has a twenty-six percent share of the listening market! Screw up again, and I'll mouse you a good one.'

'Seriously? You'll punch me? Something tells me your boyfriends don't stick around for long.'

'None of your damn business,' she said. 'Follow me. I want to show you something.'

We crossed back over the North Bridge, this time heading toward Old Town. Edinburgh has a New Town and an Old Town. The New Town is new in the same way that the New Testament is new. The Old Town was built when the Old Testament was still a first draft. (There you go, my first Edinburgh joke!) Marlene made a pointless zigzag, and we reached a wending close, bordered on both sides by great, uneven slabs of stone. Lugging my suitcase up the wide footworn steps, I saw that every square inch of wall was slathered with posters, and every poster was slathered with stars, and every star heralded an inflated superlative: *Delightful! Astonishing! Side-splitting! Mesmerizing!* It was like Zimbabwean currency.

'Brace yourself!' Marlene said, and we emerged onto The Royal Mile.

Suddenly we were besieged by feral hordes of the theatrically dispossessed: malformed Richard the Thirds, sallow-eyed Sweeney Todds, ragamuffin Sally Bowles, Grizabellas, Fagins, Tevyas, costumed ghouls. They clutched at leaflets, proffering them toward us in supplication. I felt a hand pawing my shoulder and turned to see a pubescent Willy Loman in a suit three sizes too large.

'Please, mister,' he pleaded in a trained baritone voice violently at odds with his acne-ridden face. 'Come see our production of *Death of a Salesman* by The American High School Productions. 3pm, Venue 48.'

'Bugger off!' Marlene yelled sharply, and he lumbered away. An improv troupe bounded toward us, and I felt a rising apprehension – not so much from what they wanted, but from the fact that they were human at all.

'We're the Whoopee Cushions. Give us a setting, any setting . . . a chiropodist's waiting room . . . a bus stop . . . anything.'

Marlene snarled, and they scampered.

A young teenage girl crumpled a flyer into my hands. 'A wheelie bin ate my sister,' she implored. It sounded like a lament. Out of pity, I took the leaflet. It was for an experimental children's theater production.

Marlene snatched it and threw it to the ground. 'Don't make eye contact, else you'll never shake them.'

'Why are we here?' I asked.

'So you can see the outer ring of hell first hand. You need to take this seriously.'

We shouldered through the desperation, discarded posters lapping at our feet – posters piled upon posters – kazoo orchestras, pan pipe ensembles, metallic human statues, crossdressers on stilts, the cast of *A Few Good Men* reimagined as an 'all gay, all hot-pants revue', and several malodorous bagpipers. The overwhelming stench of flop sweat and smoldering dreams took my breath away. I've seen real-life horror before – car crashes, crack mothers selling babies – but I'd never imagined anything as humanly abysmal as an am-dram production of *A Clockwork Orange*, and already I'd seen posters for three different productions. It occurred to me that the novels I'd been reading about schoolgirls fleeced of all innocence by a manipulative Mussolini-loving schoolmistress and AIDS-infected junkies were, by Edinburgh standards, *feel-good* stories: candy-coated fairy tales designed to paint the place in a more charitable light.

We reached the bottom of the street where a forty-foot-high inflated Perrier bottle billowed on its moorings like a zeppelin. Marlene paused. 'Are you sufficiently overwhelmed?'

'No,' I lied. 'I'm in a whole different league than this crap.'

'Why? Because of your *credits*? No one here watches *Letterman* or *The Tonight Show*.'

'No. Because I offer something more substantial to the viewing public than slipping into hot pants and yelling, "You can't handle the truth!" nightly.'

'Here's the truth: No one here knows you. Here, you're just another schmo. If you're going to rise above this' – she indicated the multitudes – 'you need to stop thinking like an American comedian.'

'What does that mean?'

'In six-minute increments, in *talk show* segments.'

'I have *hundreds* of increments.'

'You *need* an hour. You can't afford to stumble out of the gate again like you just did. Caffeine!'

I went to a coffee shop, bought a couple of cappuccinos and did

123

some evasive editing of my past. *Why was I here again? Oh yeah, to reclaim my mojo, to find that epiphanic light.*

When I came back, Marlene was perched somewhat primly on my suitcase, passing out flyers. I shook my head.

'Beggary,' I said. 'Beggary and desperation.'

'More effective than you think.' A male passer-by approached. Marlene shot a flyer at him so adroitly, the gentleman appeared to grab it as a measure of self-defense. Ten yards further along, he tossed it on the pavement. I watched this with no small disconsolation.

'What's the point?' I asked. 'They just get chucked.'

'That's why I printed your picture on both sides. People trample all over your face, but at least they see it.'

I took one from her and read a description of myself, a summation of my 'style of humor', a list of credits, a blurb from David Letterman that I'd made up. 'I feel like I'm reading my own obituary.'

'You will be if you blow another press interview.' She thumbed her glasses back up her face. 'Listen, have a high old time. Drink till sunup with all your comedy buddies. Chase the local talent. Whatever.' She waved a dismissive hand as if to indicate such behavior was beneath her. 'But understand, for me this isn't summer camp. I'm committed to one thing: putting asses in seats. For you.'

'Okay, Marlene.' She was starting to get on my nerves.

'Thus, when I present opportunities – particularly *media* opportunities – that might impact on our success, I expect more than the cavalier attitude you have just exhibited. Any questions?'

'Just one: did you ever consider buying glasses that fit?'

'Very funny. You think I don't own a sense of humor?'

'You're Austrian.'

'C'mon, I'll show you your flat.'

We trundled back through the Old Town. Whisky shops, tartan suppliers, shortbread merchants, heraldry investigators. I was having a hard time deciding if this was Scottish authenticity or theme-park fantasia. The crowds began to thin out. We passed a corner police precinct, reached an embankment and the scenery changed so abruptly, I needed a neck brace. We were overlooking a vivid, anomalous volcanic plug rising from a scroll of green meadow. 'Arthur's Seat,' Marlene announced. 'Stimulating climb if you're up for it.'

It was otherworldly, and I could have stared at it for hours, but Marlene was already spurring toward an enclave of flats about a hundred yards away. I chased along. She fumbled with some keys and pushed through an ornamental gate. We treaded a pathway bordered by bog myrtle and arrived at a humorless-looking flat with a sagging portico that seemed to serve no purpose whatsoever.

'What are your standards of comfort?' she asked. Before I could answer, we were standing in the front room. I looked around and said, 'I've never seen the point of tassels on furniture.'

'This place actually belongs to Lord Steele. Scottish Baron,' she announced, implying this was some sort of coup. 'Big parliamentarian doo-dah. Apparently, he uses it for illegal raves.'

'Must be some real debauchery,' I replied, noting the engravings of hawks on the wall and a somewhat startling portrait of Princess Margaret anointing an Ayrshire bull with a blue ribbon. I set my suitcase down and went over to a window that looked out directly onto the amazing mountain.

'It'll do. In fact, it's fantastic.'

'I'm across town if you need me,' she said, somewhat non-specifically. 'There's an off-license across from the police station. Follow the embankment and you'll find a small park full of escalating ethnic conflict but with pleasant bench views of the Seat.' She dropped a folder onto the coffee table. 'Your schedule. We've got more press in the morning. I'll knock.' Then she was gone – God knows where.

I unpacked my suitcase, all the while thinking about the evisceration I'd just been dragged through. I went back to the window and watched the mountain darkening against the Hibernian sky. I wondered what Marlene did with her nights. I pictured her in a dirndl, propping up the end of a schnapps bar, looking for trouble.

From a phone on the bedside table, I dialed Jim Rose in Seattle. I was thinking about the cockroach incident earlier that evening.

Jim was a con artist, a fabulist and the impresario of the freak collective known as the *Jim Rose Circus*. His French wife, BeBe, was part of the ensemble. We'd known each other from our days as street performers. Now they toured with Nine Inch Nails, headlined Lollapalooza, packed festivals all over the world. Jim was a master of media stunts and when I'd heard the cockroach story, I'd recognized his fingerprints all over it.

'Hello!'

'*Varnished croissant . . .?*'

'Who's this?'

'Rich Hall.'

'Rich-ee how ya' doing! You're in Edinburgh?'

I told him that I'd been in the studio when his wife called in with her little sabotage act.

'They're ripping us off, Rich-ee. Have you seen the poster? The asshole swallowing the scorpion?'

'I did.'

'I was doing that in 1989! These Japanese fucksticks are regurgitating my propwash.' I could picture him in his black attire, his impish Van Dyke beard, characteristically wired. 'The bane of a true artist is to suffer at the hands of chiselers, miscreants and impostors.'

'Who said that?'

'Leonardo Rembrandt, I don't know. You selling any tickets?'

'A few.'

'Rich-ee . . . you need *media*, friend. How about this . . . what if I arrange to have Lemmy from Motörhead punch you? Like, right on the Royal Mile. In front of the *Edinburgh Evening News*. I know the editor.' Everyone seemed to know the editor of the *Edinburgh Evening News.*

'I don't think I want to be punched by Lemmy from Motörhead.'

'It'll be fake. You put a blood capsule in the mouth. That kind of shit sells tickets.'

'I appreciate that Jim, but I'm easing myself in. I don't even know what I'm gonna do for an hour.'

'Trust me. The hour you don't have is funnier than most of the drivel passing itself off as entertainment up there. British comedians all think they're class warriors. The Irish think they're drunken poets. And the Australians think sound effects are hilarious. They're all trying to be *profound* or some shit. Just be funny. Follow your muse.'

'Thanks for the advice, Jim.'

'Lenny Bruce invented stand-up comedy in 1958. While he was on heroin.'

'I know, Jim. I gotta go. Long distance and all. Give BeBe my best.'

'Okay Rich-ee. Kick some ass for me.'

'Will do.'

Opening night. My venue was a fireplace. Walk-in-sized, but a fireplace, nonetheless. It was in a lecture room on the second floor of the Edinburgh University Student Union. Portable stage, a transom of lights and eighty plastic chairs.

In fact, the room wasn't disappointing. Something about its academic staidness seemed to elevate the whole notion of comedy. On the mantle above the fireplace sat a statuette by Le Corbusier. When I thought about the club logos I'd performed in front of – a flamingo clutching a microphone, a cross-eyed peanut, a solicitous banana – this place seemed dignified.

I went onstage and, within five minutes, fused with an initially recalcitrant audience in that same way they say an old cowboy is part of his horse. The terrain was different, but the footings, the turns, the instincts were the same. I stumbled now and then, but the secret is in the recovery. The thirty-seven people who had shown up laughed loud and hard, went away thoroughly entertained, and I felt like a new world had opened up to me for the simple reason that my craft had so narrowed. Let me put it another way: I killed.

Afterward, Marlene led me upstairs to a dining hall, a great oaken emporium with a vast bar at one corner. The room had been converted into a venue with a small stage at the far end of the room, tucked menacingly underneath a balcony. Marlene motioned me to a table and presented me with copious notations of what had worked and what hadn't, what I should keep and what I should throw out.

'I don't know, Marlene. I might try all different stuff tomorrow.' Annoyance crossed her face. I changed the subject: 'How about a *wee* dram of whisky? Maybe two?' I really *was* feeling celebratory.

'Club soda,' she said curtly.

I came back with a club soda and a double Glenmorangie. I wafted the single malt under my nose in that way people do to signify I don't know what. I downed it and felt it wash over me like a warm wave.

'That's the most satisfying show I've done in years!' I half-shouted.

'It needs order,' she said. 'You seem to want to be a gunslinger. How do we resolve this?'

'Give me time to think about that.' I waved my glass. 'I'm having another of these.'

I went back to the bar and ordered another double, noting the rhythmic movement of figures beginning to fill the room. I looked over at the stage and saw that it was now lit up.

'What's the show?' I asked the barman.

'Berr-put,' he replied, rolling the word like a marble.

'Bearpit?'

'Aye, tha's why saed.'

I was beginning to see there are two distinct accents in Edinburgh: *Miss Jean Brodie* and *Trainspotting*. You gotta keep your ears peeled.

I went back to the table. 'What's the Bearpit?' I asked Marlene.

'Late-night slugfest.'

'I want to go on.'

'I thought so.'

Marlene went off in search of the promoter. I went back to the bar for another double.

The show started up, and I understood immediately why it was called the Bearpit. The audience was an enraged animal and the acts who took the stage were there solely to provoke it.

A collegiate-looking man in a corduroy jacket went up and began reading a poem.

'Imagine Amsterdam . . .' he intoned. But we couldn't. Nor could we imagine what made him think that what we desired in the way of late-night entertainment was a poem. 'Its houses a-tilt, like David Bowie's teeth . . .'

Someone from the overhanging balcony emptied a beer onto his head. Undaunted, he pressed on. 'The fury of its secrets . . .'

'The Frankness of its Anne!' someone yelled back.

Overwhelmed by my love for that sterling heckle, I lustily ordered my fourth double.

The hapless poet was followed by a duo in matching denim who called themselves Girls With Big Jests. (This was 1995, and there was still such a thing as irony.) The girls had a cloying habit of touching their foreheads together when they delivered a joke. This agitated the crowd, which snarled without ever taking a breath, a bubbling continuous drone. The girls withered and ran offstage after five minutes.

I was introduced.

I walked toward the stage with the distinct sense of being evaluated before I even reached the mike. The emcee had said I was from

Montana. Before I opened my mouth, someone from the crowd yelled, 'Dental floss!'

I immediately recognized this as an arcane reference to a Frank Zappa song and congratulated the man on his musical tastes. You have to know the difference between a heckle and drunken disassociation. Then, an opening line: 'This seems to be a very paranoid city. I went into a sandwich shop and said to the lady behind the counter, "Can I have a crab-salad sandwich?" She said, "We're all out of crab-salad, I'm afraid".'

The joke landed like a satisfying chunk of meat. The beast wolfed it down, sat back on its haunches and waited for another. I fed it another. And another. I rocketed through the set to a rousing ovation and came offstage feeling invincible. *Grizzly Man*, I said to myself. *I'm the fucking Grizzly Man.*

Back at the table, Marlene was scribbling notes onto a pad.

'Put the pen down, Marlene. I don't need my jokes tabulated.' She dropped the pen and shrugged. I think I detected a small acquiescence behind her glasses. 'Do you ever relax?'

She glanced around.

'You suppose this bar serves schnapps?' she asked.

I can't say I sobered up for the entire month. Yet, that's not to say I stayed drunk. It was something else: I was afloat on the inebriation of invention. Edinburgh accommodated the two things I'm good at: lying and forgetting. All jokes are manipulative, and audiences laugh when you reach a truthful kernel within the lie. I had all day to make up those lies. And as for memory, the Fringe was not continuous with the real world. It was like one of those globe paperweights: you shook it and it snowed leaflets. All that mattered was *The Hour*, the adrenalized rush of the nightly performance in muzzy contrast to the forceful clarity of the daytime.

I wrote furiously and tore through my notebooks, never repeating the same show twice. I couldn't remember what I'd done the previous night, nor did it matter. I had so many jokes and ideas, I took to marking them on individual slices of Kraft American Cheese. This was in lieu of a Rolodex. Eventually, I arranged the slices on a wooden board and brought them up onstage. I would have someone in the audience throw a dart. Wherever the dart landed, that's where the show went. It drove Marlene crazy.

I'd wake up at midday with a half-formed idea. By five o'clock, it was an obsession. By night, it became aerial. Sometimes it worked, sometimes it didn't. The night I attempted to build a replica of the Scott Memorial from cereal packets: less than stellar. The crowd filed out, I stood in the rubble of Cornflakes and Coco Pops, and Marlene reflected desultorily that maybe I needed to start searching elsewhere for inspiration.

'You can't buy your entire act from Morrisons,' she said.

When I wasn't performing comedy, I was thinking about comedy, and when I wasn't thinking about comedy, I was absorbing comedy. I studied tons of other comedians. Some were revelations. Dylan Moran, an Irishman, could have been the template for Jim Rose's crack about 'drunken poets'. He was disheveled, precariously dangling the mike in front of his face like he was trying to find his house key at three in the morning. But behind the façade was a consummate imagist, shambling about the stage, painting exquisite word-pictures and conjuring phrases with masterful nonchalance. I tried to imagine an American comic trying that approach. They would have come off too pleased with themselves.

Bill Bailey changed my view of musical comedy. In the States, musical comedy was a guy with a guitar sending up *American Pie*. Bill was an original. He dressed all in black. His hair could only be described as a mullet that had given up its dream of being a mullet. And he was astoundingly talented. He would hunch over a piano and deconstruct a classical piece, reducing it to intellectual blasphemy, then wander across the stage, pick up a Telecaster and launch into a full-throttled, mini-rock opera with a chorus of 'Human slaves! In an insect nation!' It was like watching a roadie left to his own devices, knowing the band was already on the bus headed back to the Marriott.

The simple beauty of the Fringe was that it reduced comedy to its transactional core. No flashing marquees, no two-drink-minimums, no jalapeño poppers, no flurry of credit cards waving at the show's end like sails at sunset. You bought a ticket and a pint, walked into a sweltering room and hoped to God that someone would entertain you. Nothing slick about it. Americans want comedy that's packaged and apportioned, like Kraft American Cheese. They want the veneer, the manufactured persona. Brits want to see the human behind the jokes. They like seeing how deftly you can dig a hole and climb out of it. Me, I can dig more holes than a prairie dog on a golf course. Bring it on!

American punchlines often end with an exclamation point. Too many of mine ended in question marks: 'How come, if you can play guitar and harmonica at the same time, like Neil Young or Bob Dylan, you're a genius? But, if you make that extra effort to strap some cymbals to your knees, people will cross the street to avoid you?' That sort of thing. That joke seldom worked in America. Brits got it. Was it possible that maybe I had spent my last seventeen years doing the right comedy for the wrong people?

There is an epiphanic light we all strive for: the floodlights that bathe a grand old city, or an idea-lightbulb coming on above your head. I would stand at the window of my flat and gaze at Arthur's Seat. The mountain, or perhaps the *light* behind it, had a strange magnifying effect on the figures moving up and down its slope. It was a trick of optics, of course. As were stars, reviews, awards, accolades and platitudes: those shiny Fringe baubles that kept a monoculture at arm's length from each other. I spent a lot of late nights at the Assembly Rooms on George Street. It burbled with comedians, actors, musicians, producers, agents, publicists, all drinking and chatting blearily, making pacts with the devil, sizing each other up. You could tell when someone had gotten a good review. They'd walk into the room, and you could practically see the quotation marks coming off them.

A *Scotsman* vendor named Claude would show up on the pavement in front of the Assembly Rooms every night. The *Scotsman* carried the daily reviews. Under pretense of fresh air or a cigarette, comics would sneak out, buy a copy and furiously scan it for their names, then toss it into a nearby bin. Claude would retrieve the paper and resell it to the next furtive comedian. He must have cleaned up.

I bought the *Scotsman* every night. Why wouldn't I? Never believe a comedian who says he doesn't care about reviews. The bulk of response to our efforts is indecipherable laughter. If someone wants to translate that into meaning, I want to fucking read about it.

Claude never bothered to ask your name. That would have been bad for his business.

'How's it going, Claude?' I said one night.

'Get ready for confetti, Rich Hall,' he said. I opened the paper and saw a five-star review. That savvy Claude, pretending not to know anyone's name. He knew *everybody's* name.

I went back inside the Assembly Rooms, quietly elated. But in no time, people were coming up to congratulate me. A tray of single malts appeared. I raised my hand to bring this to a stop, but it had the opposite effect.

What the hell, I thought, knocking back a Glenfiddich, *it's not every night you get a five-star review. In fact – bartender, another round please!* Actually, I'd never gotten a review in my life. Who in America reviews comedy? One more way the Fringe – *Cheers, everyone!* – legitimized stand-up, elevated it to an art form.

I leaned on the bar, soaking up the eternal camaraderie of the room and spotted a redhead I'd met a week earlier on some radio show. She was perched on the edge of a couch, talking to a group of theater-types, waving her cocktail about like a friendly weapon. I couldn't remember if she was the host of the show or another guest, but I was suddenly smitten. Fortified by stars, I set out across the room to approach her.

I was blindsided by a huge arm that wrapped itself around my neck, hurled me downward and sent my drink glass clattering across the floor. I looked up and at the end of the arm was Lemmy from Motörhead. Muttonchops, leather cowboy hat, tiny spinning tachometers where his eyeballs should have been.

'Jim Rose said I should twat you,' he offered by way of an introduction, and flashed his teeth. He looked like a Montana trucker on speed. 'I saw your show. You're one funny cunt.'

'Thanks, Lemmy.' *Man, the accolades just keep coming.*

He seemed to have intuited where I was going and dragged me in a headlock toward the redhead and her cohorts, where he more or less used me as a battering ram to crash the proceedings.

'This is Rich Hall. Funny Yank cunt. I'm Lemmy!'

He demanded shots all around. It was unclear who this order was directed at, but shots materialized. Lemmy knocked two back in a synchronized sweep and proceeded to hold court. He had forgotten he still had me in the headlock. My neck was getting sore but, because I couldn't for the life of me think of one Motörhead song I'd ever heard, I accepted it as fitting punishment. The redhead rose from the couch, came over and extricated me like a heifer caught in barbed wire. She had startling green eyes.

'What's a big Motörhead song?' I asked under my breath.

'Ace of Spades.'

'This guy is terrifying.'

She rested her hand on my arm as a consoling gesture, maybe something more. Jocelyn. Her name was Jocelyn.

More shots.

Things blurred. Lemmy's presence dominated the room and he

was full of frightening propositions. I sort of drifted in and out of these convolutions as I was trying to make inroads with Jocelyn. At some point the disturbing notion of 'carpet-skinning Helen' was suggested. I took this to mean some kind of satanic ritual sacrifice was being proposed: I wasn't really into the death-metal scene.

'What's he talking about?' I asked Jocelyn.

'Carpet-skiing in Hillend. It's an artificial slope outside of town. He wants to take us skiing.'

'*Now?*'

'He says he knows the owner.'

We might, in fact, have gone carpet-skiing. I honestly don't remember. I hazily recall pouring out of the room en masse, falling into a black cab, Jocelyn curled up against me. The Edinburgh Castle floated past like a phantom-lit ship, floodlights shone silvery on the abutments, headlights fluttered, streetlamps wobbled, a faint moon hung over Arthur's Seat, stars, stars, stars, stars, stars, then blackness.

I awoke the following morning in a suite at the Balmoral Hotel, beside Jocelyn, with Lemmy banging on a bass guitar in the next room. Or maybe I awoke next to a bass guitar with Lemmy banging Jocelyn in the next room. One of those configurations anyway. I stumbled downstairs through the gilded Balmoral lobby, admiring the tartan furnishings and crisp, discreet-looking staff. I felt rotten – not for anything I'd done, but for what I couldn't remember. The night before had been about as much loss of control as I could stand.

Outside, it was blistering hot and every step back to my flat seemed uphill.

Marlene was waiting under the portico, jackhammering her glasses against her face, prefiguring disgust, I assumed. Instead, she bounded forth, waving the *Scotsman*. 'Five stars!'

'You don't say,' I said and spent just enough time pretending to read it so as not to appear too interested. 'You want some coffee? Come in.'

Inside, she pushed past me and whirled straight to the kitchen. 'I'll make it. Sit down and listen to what I have to say.'

I took a seat on the couch.

'We're going to be sold out from now on!' she shouted, slamming a cabinet door. 'Possibility of extra shows, maybe a bigger venue. Where do you keep the coffee!'

'By the toaster.'

'In the meantime, you're going to have promoters, managers, press, all kinds of ruminants sniffing about. I only ask that you honor your commitments and be a gentleman about it.'

'Of course.'

'Where's the milk . . . cream . . . there's nothing in this fridge but Kraft cheese.'

'You gotta take it black.'

She came back in with two coffees in clear mugs, set them down and went about the room opening windows, straightening picture frames, organizing the remote controls in ascending order of size, all with a kind of absent-minded frenzy.

'Will you sit the hell down, Marlene? Why are you so antsy?'

She propped herself on the edge of a chair and pushed up her glasses.

'The Perrier panel is in tonight.'

'Oh. That thing.'

'That *thing*? That *thing* is *critical*. What do I have to do to get you to tighten up your show?'

'Come on, Marlene . . .'

'You can't be going off on tangents that go nowhere. Not tonight.'

'Tangents? Did you read the review? "High-wire act," they called me – a high-wire act, as in working without a net.'

'You need a net. Tonight, you need a net.'

'Marlene, trust me. I can't just phone it in. That just makes me another . . . Isn't this whole festival about taking chances? Isn't that what *fringe* means?'

She stared at me. 'I thought you'd know better than that.' Then: 'Do you want to win this award or not?'

I did. No point in lying to myself. I'd bought into the false economy. Deep inside me, there is constant war between feigned detachment and a desperate desire for validation. I just didn't want to admit it – not to her, not to anyone. I wanted to be thought of as the high-wire act, grizzly killer, gunslinger. That's American comics for you: persona, not perception.

'I know you're not dumb enough to think I brought you here out of some Samaritan concern for your artistic integrity,' she said. 'I want to make the best show possible. I want remuneration. I want to make a name for myself. And I get that you're here to lose yours – or rather what generally follows it: *sniglets*. But you leave this festival with a buzz around you, and we can tour theaters. Not your shit clubs, like in America.'

'Real theaters?'

'With plush velvet seating. Where no one gives a monkey's about your damned *sniglets*.' She narrowed her eyes. 'Are you going to screw me over?'

I took a gulp of coffee and regarded her through the bottom of the mug. It softened her features. For some reason, I thought about Miss Jean Brodie and her abiding sense of betrayal. 'No Marlene. I'm not going to screw you over.'

'Alright then,' she said. She got up and wandered into the bedroom, in search of the bathroom, I assumed. I went over to the open window to get some breeze. It was the hottest day of the summer. I stared out at the Seat and thought, *I'm going to nail this award.*

Marlene had gone quiet and, when I went into the bedroom, she was lying with her glasses resting on her chest. She opened an eye and squinted. 'You mind? I'm knackered. I was out all night.'

'Yeah? Where'd you go?'

She closed her eye. 'Oh, you know ... same planet, different orbit ...'

She fell asleep.

The Scots may have invented the telephone, linoleum and mouthwash, but they've never heard of air con. My venue that night was a furnace, crammed with decent humans who had no right to be subjected to this kind of torture.

Marlene had bought a fan to put onstage, but I refused it. The crowd's suffering, I maintained, would be my suffering too. And suffer we did. No one even clapped when I came onstage – that would have required exertion. They sat with limbs extended as if they were trying to divine a breeze. Those standing splayed themselves against the wall, desperately trying to extract moisture by osmosis. Nothing in the way of humor could alleviate the misery. My jokes hit the wall of heat, died in their tracks, and any chance I had of winning over that Perrier panel quickly evaporated – as did the pints of lager, water and Irn-Bru people had brought in, foolishly thinking it would sustain them.

After about ten minutes, the crowd seemed horrified by something going on behind me. I turned and saw that the cheese board had turned to fondue. The spotlight had melted it, and a puddle of yellow effluent was slowly inching toward my feet. What was I supposed to do now? The idea of asking an audience member to throw a dart at a grid of empty cellophane squares was not, I surmised, going to be viewed as *high-wire* entertainment in anyone's book.

Still, I pressed on. My mouth turned dry. I was dehydrated and hungover and deadened inside. *You should have cancelled this show,* I thought to myself, *but no . . . You thought you'd impress the Perrier people. You thought you'd nail that little spray-painted bottle.*

Finally, in a pique of what I can only describe as monumentally misplaced resentment, I said, 'I understand the Perrier judges are in tonight . . .'

The room stiffened. At the back, by the sound desk, I saw Marlene blanch. Apparently, it was bad form to call attention to this.

'By any chance, did you assholes bring any of it with you? Because I'm fucking dying up here.'

Afterward, we found a concrete bench in front of the Student Union. I went over to a beer concession and ordered a pint, and a liter of water for Marlene. I came back, sat down and downed my drink. I think it was the best pint I'd ever tasted in my life.

'Sorry, Marlene,' I said, and I meant it. 'There was no way that situation was going to work. You know that, right?'

'No. I don't know that.' She looked defeated. I supposed she had some kind of professional relationship with the Perrier people, and I wondered if I'd ruined it.

'I was delirious,' I said. As an explanation, it didn't weigh much.

'That's how it goes,' she said. 'One minute you're creaming the opposition, then . . . gone in the next reel.'

I wasn't going to stand for that. 'You know,' I said, 'I had a high-school baseball coach like you once. He thought he could strip me of all dignity and reassemble me from scratch . . .'

'I didn't reassemble you.'

'Didn't work. We went oh-and-twenty. Now he sells discount golf equipment. I got famous, and he got fat.'

At that exact moment someone yelled, '*Sniglets!*'

I looked past Marlene and spotted an American couple approaching. Unmistakable. They had the classic never-met-a-stranger look on their faces and matching organized tour windbreakers.

The man slapped me on the shoulder. 'You,' he said, 'we see Friday.'

'Saturday,' the wife corrected. She held out a Fringe program, implying an autograph.

I did the slapping the pockets thing. 'I haven't got a pen.'

'You gotta pen, Verna?'

The wife reached inside her windbreaker and unzipped one of those travel purses you buy at the airport because all foreigners are out to rob you.

'I've got a pen,' said Marlene, who was nothing if not efficient.

We watched them walk off. It was dusk now. A streetlamp came on. Two startled cats shot out from the shadows and pinwheeled past our feet.

After a moment, I said to Marlene, 'About those theaters . . .'

'Theaters?'

'The tour, a theater tour.'

'What about it?'

'I'm thinking, do we *have* to start out with the plush velvet seating? Isn't there something a little more . . . down-market?'

She pushed her glasses up.

'Leave it to me,' she answered.

INTERLUDE 2

THE MALICK SHOT

One thing I always knew – buried deep and steadfast in my psyche, sure as shootin' and right as rain: come the day I would meet my future wife, it wouldn't be through clever bar chat-up, wowing her from a stage, a chance encounter at an elegant party, or on the internet, nor at an awards ceremony, an airline departure lounge or a dimly lit Parisian café. All viable scenarios for the flare of passion, admittedly. But not my destiny. No, no, no. I would meet the love of my life the old-school way: she would be bathing naked in a river, and I would be staring at her on horseback through some trees.

Blessed with this intuition, I probably should have spent more time near rivers and certainly more time in the saddle. Instead, I'd energetically run up a lifetime of sputtering relationships doomed to end in emotional stalemate. And every time I looked back at why love had failed, the answer was patently obvious: when I first met these women, *they* had not been bathing naked in a river, and *I* had not been on horseback staring at them through some trees.

Thus, it should come as no surprise that when I first encountered Karen – the woman I married and am still married to, mother of my children, whose equanimity and strength of mind steadies my rocky course through life, whose discretion allows me to be who I am, but who also quite willfully nailed a Post-it Note to my head to remind me that my years of sleeping in late, drinking too much, Harley-Davidsons, one-night stands, three-day fishing trips, going out when I want, coming home when I please, peeing off my own front porch, and blasting Neil Young and Crazy Horse through JBL speakers at three in the morning were officially *kaput* – she was partially submerged, and I was mounted.

July 12, 2003. The Trossachs. It was blistering hot for Scotland. Loch Katrine's surface calm made its stark, cold depth deceptive. Fishermen, the victims of violent squalls that could spring up on this stretch of water without warning, were buried beneath our boat. But right now, the sun was low over the western slope of the lake, bathing an undifferentiated line of trees in warm-hued light – what cinematographers call the 'golden hour', when everything looks nostalgic and permeated with a sense of lost innocence. This, of course, served no purpose whatsoever to the scene Mike Wilmot and I were filming, in which Mike eats carp bait.

We were making a BBC comedy series called *Rich Hall's Fishing Show*. The premise was an action fishing show where – in the span of six half-hour episodes – Mike and I uniformly fail to catch a single fish. Thus, each segment was filled with quasi-philosophical ramblings, recreational mishaps and shoreline encounters with an increasingly bizarre host of characters: Charles Manson as a ceiling fan salesman, the disembodied head of a limousine driver, what have you.

The camera and crew were positioned almost a quarter-mile away, shooting from the framed window of a centuries-old Georgian guest-house built on the side of a crowned ridge, which dropped down a pebbly slope to the edge of the gorgeous green loch. The director Chris Cottam's idea was to start wide, pull focus, push across the watery divide and arrive at an extreme close-up of our faces. There was a two-way radio lying on the floor of the boat. Chris cackled 'Action!' and we went for the eleventh take of the afternoon.

'Mike,' I said, 'you're the carp expert. What have we got today?'

'Well, Rich. I've brought boilies – or fish balls, as we call them in Canada.' Mike pulled a clear plastic bag from the tackle box and extracted a crusty, marble-sized bolus with thumb and forefinger. He held it in front of his face. 'It's a mixture of bird-seed and fishmeal. Personally, I like to coat mine with Marmite as a scent promulgator – can we see this at home? About two dozen of these will get you through an entire day of carp fishing.'

Then he popped the boilie into his mouth and ate it.

Even after the eleventh go, it still cracked me up. Something about the insouciant way he threw it down his gullet, followed by a thin, chronic smile to camera. He's one of the naturally funniest guys I've ever met.

We waited to hear 'Cut' from the radio. Silence. Mike picked it up and pushed the talk button. 'How was that? Anybody? Hello!'

'Give us a sec,' we heard Chris say.

'C'mon, that was perfect,' Mike barked. 'Tell us you got that.' His face was sunburnt, his angler's costume – multi-pocket shirt, quick-dry khakis – mottled with sweat. The ensemble looked all wrong on him, although in comedy, that's generally an asset. He was a city-bred Torontonian with a wide face and a physique that immediately made you think *He should take better care of himself*, evidenced by at least two-dozen Marlboro Light butts scattered on the floor of the boat.

We waited. No reply. Mike fired up a cigarette and took one drag.

'Enough. I'm taking us in,' he announced. He gave the pressure bulb on the gas line a squeeze and the outboard started on the first pull. Suddenly, the radio crackled.

'Turn that engine off!'

Mike picked up the radio. 'What, Chris, *what*? That last take was stellar. I got beer waiting for me.'

'One more,' Chris said.

Mike seldom got riled, but right now he was. 'Alright, just shoot it, chrissake.'

'Patience,' Chris answered.

Mike killed the engine and sat back down on the transom. '*Patience?* What the hell is he waiting for?'

I knew exactly. I gestured for the radio.

'Chris,' I called, 'lemme guess – you're waiting for the light.'

'Roger. You two never looked sexier. This is the Terrence Malick shot, guys. Seriously, give it one more minute.' Then he abruptly cut contact.

'Hear that? He wants his Terrence Malick moment.' I stared at Mike. 'Know what? You actually look pretty damn fetching right now.'

'Oh stop with yo' sattidy night talkin',' he replied.

I set the radio down, picked up an oar and racked it across my shoulders, arms draped over each end: the Martin Sheen pose from *Badlands*. The radio squawked back to life.

'What are you guys doing? Positions!'

'Just roll,' I said. I was body-miked, and I knew the soundman would convey the message. I turned, taking a dramatic 360-degree sweep of the stunning backdrop, aligned myself to the guest house and began talking: 'This is what they call the golden hour and our director, Chris Cottam, has asked for a Terrence Malick moment. That would be the Terrence Malick who directed *Days of Heaven* and *Badlands*. Now, a Malick film generally deals with epic themes like morality, temptation, love and the confluence of grace and nature. A verdant state of being, if you will.'

Mike had picked up on where this was going and was now pronated across the transom, gazing fixedly into the distance: an approximation of the painting *Christina's World* by Andrew Wyeth.

'Understandably,' I continued, 'any director would be seduced by these optics and desire to capture the moment in all its translucence. The only problem is, this is a comedy fishing show, we're hot and thirsty, this boat stinks of fish balls. I'm not Martin Sheen, the Canuck behind me is not Sissy Spacek and our director – whose previous assignment was an advert for a string of discount shoe outlets – is most definitely not, nor will ever be, Terrence Fucking

Malick. So, enjoy the vista, folks, because that's all you're getting out of this scene.'

'Cut and wrap, guys,' came Chris's voice over the radio. 'That was spectacular. I've got tears in my eyes. Also, I'll have you know, that shoe commercial paid for my house.'

Mike started up the outboard and we puttered back to shore.

At the boathouse, a transport runner, a gangly kid with sunken features and a distinct lack of social cognizance, was waiting for us. He made no effort to throw us a line. Mike missed the dock and rammed the boat into some reeds, unleashing a canopy of midges and horseflies.

'Good one. Another eggshell landing,' I said, slapping at bugs.

'Screw it. You park the damn thing.' Mike clambered over the gunwale, sank into muck and had to flail himself toward dry ground like the *Creature from the Black Lagoon*, leaving it for me to reverse the boat and get it over to the dock.

We had no idea if the runner was Scots, English or a mute. He just led us wordlessly to a waiting golf cart. We jumped on and headed up a dirt track toward the guesthouse, skirting the waterline with its great green hummocks of liverwort and vibrant blue flag iris. We were facing backward and the alpenglow sky, the trees, the water – everything – was like brushwork: a master stroke, plein air painting. It was a truly astonishing time of day, made all the more astonishing when I looked to my left, through a stand of hazel trees, and observed a woman bathing in a cove.

If you try to analyze your actions, they own you. Better to act on your impulses. If you're not meant for *something*, it follows that you are not meant for *anything*. I knew, absolutely, I was meant for this moment, even though, technically, I wasn't on horseback. But when I leapt off the back of the golf cart, I noted it was called a Pinto. Fair enough. Also, she was in a lake, not a river. Again, a minor concession to destiny.

For a long time, I just stood and watched her through the branches. She was waist-deep in the water, wearing only a bra, luminous against her thrilling figure. Not for one second did it occur to me, for all intents, I was a pervert. She dug her fingers into her scalp, pushed them up through her blonde hair, which loosened and fell in a marvelous declaration of . . . I can't quite say. The end of a sweltering day? Splendid isolation?

She looked up and spotted me. 'Rich Hall. We've met before.'

'I don't think so,' I said. 'I would have remembered.'

'Well, we have.'

I suppose it was true. Her name was Karen, and she was a production assistant for Open Mike Productions, the parent company making our show. I'd caught a few fleeting glimpses of her around the offices in London but couldn't for the life of me remember actually being introduced.

'Are you going to stand there like a deviant, or are you going to come in?' she called.

If it had been normal light, I might very well have demurred. I'm not much for skinny-dipping in the chill of northern waters. It might be therapeutic, but it's a shock to the system and takes some real getting used to – not unlike marriage. (Maybe that's why they call it 'taking the plunge'.) But in this moment, everything was diffused. It was the golden hour. Also, I reeked of fish balls and needed a good rinse.

I dove in.

She came to my shows. We chatted in bars. Went to parties together. Each of these occasions, I like to think, raised her estimation of me. I wanted to tell her that I really, really fancied her, but that would have contained meaning and subjected me to overexposure. I was happy enough just to be in her company, a presence that cancelled any further expectation.

Then, one night, sitting outside a pizza joint on Tottenham Court Road in London, I just came out with it. Told her I wanted to spend all my time with her. That I knew from the instant I first saw her – in that Terrence Malick moment – she was the *Days of Heaven* to my *Badlands*. I left it at that because I was starting to sound like a bad song.

Hearing these words, she smiled. It was a warm September night. The fluorescence from the pizza sign was harsh, but it didn't matter. She looked great in any light.

Finally, she said: 'Terrence who?'

'Malick.'

'Not familiar with the name,' she said, picking up the menu. 'Well, now, let's see what looks good.'

CHAPTER 5

THE NIGHT
OF THE RICH HALLS

January in the early 2000s. Hudson Hotel. New York City. Roughly, the midpoint of a transatlantic relationship that spans from the UK to a small Montana town. Karen was washing her hands rather dramatically in the bathroom while I alligator-wrestled her suitcase. She was flying back to London, and I could already see weight-allowance issues at JFK.

The phone rang. She came into the room, slathered in shea butter or lanolin or some other jungle effluent. 'You're not going to answer that?'

'Probably just housekeeping,' I said.

She threw a hand towel onto the bed and picked up the receiver.

'Hi, Ad. He's right here.' She handed the phone over, gestured she would meet me in the lobby and left, trailing the vapor of the tropics behind her.

It was Addison Cresswell, my agent in London.

157

'You're 2,000 words short, guv,' he said brusquely. I could picture him pacing the floorboards of his office, eyes bearing straight forward: a phone pugilist.

'That's not possible. I came in at 65,000.'

'Your publisher's cut two chapters. Legal issues. I can fight it if you want – I'm happy to fight – but you won't make the spring release.'

I sat down on the edge of a stiff wing chair purposely designed to make people check out of hotel rooms on time.

'Which chapters did they cut?' I asked.

'Doesn't matter. Right now, it's a question of getting the cattle to Abilene, as they say.'

'Addison, stop using cowboy phrases. They don't work in an East End accent.'

'You need 2,000 words. Something wonderful right away.'

'What's *right away*?'

'Tomorrow, 10am. That's all the time I could buy you.'

'Alright, I'm thinking.'

'Nobody buys humor books in the summer.'

'Alright, Addison. I'll come up with something.'

He hung up. The clock on the bedside table said 2pm.

The book was called *Things Snowball*, a collection of comic essays – a *real* book, so to speak, and a chance to move beyond the lightweight confines of *Sniglets*. For the last six months, I had allowed it to subsume my life at the expense of emotional connections, personal safety, hygiene and any other misguided sense of civic decency. I knew Karen was fed up with me. Ignoring your partner is a form of debt accumulation and, to make up for it, I'd flown her in from London, business class. (Yeah, it was that serious.)

I dragged her around, in her jet-lagged torpor, to department stores and boutiques, watching her not buy stuff. We went to an off-Broadway revival of David Mamet's *Oleanna*, which ends with a female student being beaten almost unconscious by her professor. The girl's last words of dialogue are, 'Don't worry about me. I'm alright.' Then she lunges for his throat. Karen slept through that part. We ate dinner in Chinatown, where she discovered she was violently allergic to black forest mushrooms. In the city that never sleeps, she was up all night in the bathroom. Yessiree, a real couple's getaway.

I managed to get Karen's suitcase secured and lugged it down to the lobby. Inside a sports-themed bar on the far side of the registration desk, I spotted her nursing a medicinal Bloody Mary. I went to join her and smacked right into a plate-glass partition. It was a pointless design feature and I never saw it. Bang!

I lay on the floor staring heavenward. New Yorkers flowed past obliviously, like time itself. My vision was blurred, so I shifted my focus to a photograph of Mike Tyson on the wall until it wavered into clarity. The photo was autographed. I wondered if ol' Mike had ever walked into this glass.

Suddenly Karen's face appeared above me, her lips making a tight ring of astonishment, like someone had stolen her cigar. 'My god, honey. Are you okay?'

I muttered that I was fine, that I just wanted to lie there for a while. An idea for a story was forming in my head. If I stood up, I thought

I might lose it. The idea was this: the World Boxing Organization hears that I have withstood the glass divider at the sports bar at the Hudson. They check their records and discover that Mike Tyson, Lennox Lewis and Dariusz Michalczewski have all, at one time or another, been knocked unconscious by this very structure. My unknocked-out-by-a-plate-glass-window status is the most impressive feat in the last few anemic years of boxing. Thus, they inform me, I am scheduled to fight reigning light-heavyweight Roy Jones Jr in Atlantic City, New Jersey, in six months' time.

Karen helped me up, dusted me off and dragged her suitcase outside to the taxi rank. I stumbled behind with the movements of a lout. She turned and steadied me by the shoulders.

'Are you sure you're okay? I don't feel like I should leave you.'

'I'm fine,' I said. That wasn't quite true. For example, I noticed the bustling Manhattan street now appeared as a postcard vignette from the turn of the nineteenth century. Everything was circular and fuzzy around the edges. On the other hand, I had a great idea for a story and figured I should bump my noggin more often.

'Have a good flight,' I said. 'I'll call you in the morning.' She kissed me, and I watched her yellow cab pull away. Except now it was monochrome.

I was due to fly out to my Montana house the following afternoon for a three-days-to-kill rest before a stint of one-nighters in the Pacific Northwest. But I changed my flight and checked out a day early. I figured I would sketch the story out on the plane, then get home and fire up the keyboard.

Airborne, I think I still had a bit of tunnel vision, but it was hard to tell for sure, because I *was* in a tunnel. Somewhere over Pennsylvania, the flight attendant came down the aisle chucking complimentary Fritos bags at passengers. I tore mine open and stared out the plane window thinking, *what would I do if I were scheduled to fight Roy Jones Jr? Obviously, the man's going to kill me.*

I scribbled onto my notepad. *Devise a strategy that has worked well for a lot of boxers of late: create a hopeless muddle of legal injunctions and contractual hang-ups, which would maintain my ranking without ever actually having to set foot in the ring.*

I popped a couple of Fritos in my mouth and studied the bag. *Maybe try to wrangle some product endorsements along the way.*

Changing planes in Chicago, I hiked – forever it seemed – through a fluorescent morass of ill-tempered Midwesterners and fast-food swindlers until I reached the departure gate for Bozeman, Montana. Here the passengers looked so distinctively Western the effect was like already being home. I counted eleven cowboy hats and at least as many shearling coats. One wiry-looking young man was snoring absently in his hard plastic seat, his underslung boot-heels propped up by a saddle: carry-on luggage.

Descending into Bozeman, we encountered a bit of drama. The landing gear indicator wasn't functioning in the cockpit, so the co-pilot had to run to the back of the plane to do a visual inspection of the wheel-well. He raced down the aisle avoiding eye contact, but as he passed me his hand momentarily grabbed my shoulder, either for balance or to administer last rites. I looked out the window and saw the flashing lights of rescue vehicles tearing down the snow-covered access road leading to the airport. I was thinking, *I can't die. I have a deadline.*

I looked around at the other faces on the plane. No one looked the least bit panicked. For most of them, the City of Chicago was probably more unnerving than an emergency landing.

The plane slammed onto the runway, lurched for a few hundred yards, then smoothed itself out. I looked out the window and saw whirlpools of snow on the tarmac, everything wintry and white. Suddenly the airport crash tender appeared racing alongside us, lit up like a sporting event. I wrote: *Or perhaps, stage a tune-up match in the interim. Someone who couldn't fight their way out of a wet paper bag. Better yet, fight a wet paper bag. That could be a confidence-builder.*

The house on Clark Street in Livingston was one of those Masonite and timber-frame constructions that cropped up in the 1930s when everything was being built with pilfered railyard materials. Draped in pristine whiteness, it looked small and perfect. I kicked some snow off the front porch and felt like I was violating a cupcake. I tried my front-door key. It turned but the door wouldn't give. Someone had safety-locked it from the inside. *What the hell?* Then I remembered an email from my neighbor Mark Bolton, asking if his 'Welsh friend' could stay there for a few days while I was in New York. Mark's a fly-fishing guide and he's always got angling buddies showing up in the off season to sit around and evoke riparian memories. This had slipped my mind.

I banged on the door. No answer. I banged again. I descended the porch steps, clumped around to the back door and found it locked as well. I retraced my steps and decided the dining-room window might offer some possibility of ingress. I caught the ledge with my raw fingers and pulled myself up to eye level, scrabbling for purchase against the side of the house. Ice had formed around the panes in small bluish arcs. I got the window open and clambered onto the sill, my feet kicking at empty air. *This is what I would look like climbing back into the ring after Roy Jones Jr has ejected me with a single punch*, I thought.

I was halfway inside when a figure clad only in boxer shorts came at me with my own Emmy. He wielded it clumsily, his hand wrapped around the torso of a winged woman clutching an atom. The statuette had a heavy round base, and I believe that was the intended point of impact.

'That's an Emmy!' I shouted. 'Can you please put that down?' We Montanans tend to regard all out-of-towners with ambiguous condescension, and I wanted to tell him attacking homeowners with their own Emmys was not a thing we did here. Instead, I just said, 'For future reference, there's a baseball bat by the kitchen back door.'

He lowered the statuette and offered a handshake. 'Rich Hall. I'm Mark Bolton's friend.'

This struck me as unusually formal. I wormed the remainder of my body through the window, took the Emmy from him and returned it to the dining room shelf. Then I switched on the light.

He was a rotund guy with a ruddy unfinished-looking face, as if it had been drawn by a lazy cartoonist. He didn't seem the least self-conscious to be standing there in his boxers, which irked me somehow because, well, he was in my house. Now I would have to do laundry – bedsheets, towels – maybe a brisk fumigation.

'Mark said you wouldn't be back until tomorrow night.'

'Well, I'm a day early.'

'No need to apologize.'

'I'm not apologizing. I'm a day early in my own house.'

'No problem. I'll just gather my belongings and find a motel. I believe there are several out by the interstate.' He had a cadence that sounded like he was going to break into song at any moment. I'm sure he was a pleasant guy, but I just wasn't in the mood for chitchat.

'The Yellowstone Motor Inn has an indoor pool,' I said, probably too abruptly. 'Heated.'

'Done.'

He headed off into the bedroom. I took quick inventory of the dining room. Everything looked tidy – tidier, actually, than when I'd last been there. My desk, normally a landslide zone, had been organized into piles, pens laid side by side. I noted a red candle in a jar where no candle had been before.

He emerged from the bedroom lugging a big plaid suitcase. His black peacoat was completely inappropriate for the latitude, and I suddenly felt bad sending him out into a blizzard.

'I didn't catch your name,' I said.

'Rich Hall.'

'?'

'Didn't Mark tell you? I'm Rich Hall as well.'

'No. Actually he never brought that up.' I felt a kind of jolt go through me.

'That's Mark Bolton for you. He can tell you the Latin name for every bug on the water. He'll point to a mayfly and say, "*Ephemerella infrequens*". I'll say, "Mark, it's a mayfly. Just call it a mayfly." But I doubt if he knows his own kid's name. Ah, well. Thanks so much for the hospitality. Cheers.'

And he was gone.

I made some coffee, sat down at the desk with my notes and fired up my iMac G3, a weird contraption that resembled a cheerful, severed robot head. A blue iris pulsated, and the screen lit up. I typed: 'Much like Sugar Ray Leonard's retina, I am fairly detached when it comes to boxing.'

Solid opening. I did a quick word count. Fifteen down, 1,985 to go.

Outside, an icicle ripped from the gutter and crashed beneath the window. I got up from the desk and went over, looked out and saw ice shards dashed like test tubes against the snow. Across the street, framed in his kitchen window, I could make out Mark's silhouette. From his rhythmic, staccato movements, I could tell he was tying flies. I stood and watched for a while. The distal quality of the storm made it seem like the only people on the planet were him, me, and an errant Welshman – and *two* of us were named Rich Hall. That was really bothering me.

I went back to my desk and tried to concentrate on the story, but the question kept gnawing at me: *Why had Mark not mentioned in his email his friend's name was Rich Hall?* That's just something you would definitely bring up, as in: 'I have a friend who needs a place to stay for a few days and I was wondering if it would be okay if he crashed at yours? Get this – his name is Rich Hall as well!'

Was it possible my name was so mundane that it failed to register with people? I typed *Rich Hall* onto the screen and stared at it. Admittedly, it didn't exactly jump off the page.

Rich Hall. Rich Hall. Rich Hall. Rich Hall. Rich Hall. Rich Hall. Rich Hall.

I typed it over and over. Repetition is supposed to give rhythm and emphasis to your writing. 'O Captain! my Captain!' 'Ashes to ashes, dust to dust'. It didn't work with 'Rich Hall'. I kept staring at the words until I realized I was turning into Jack Torrance from *The Shining*. I hit delete and watched my name vaporize into blank eternity.

I checked the computer clock. It was 5am in London. Five hours to deadline.

Concentrate. Boxing. Okay . . .

I typed: 'As far as I'm concerned, the sport lost its luster the day George Foreman started peddling his cheese grill.'

I read it back.

'Luster'? 'Lustre'! C'mon, man, think British. The precious seconds it takes a typesetter to Anglicize that word could mean the difference between a spring release and summer. You never see someone lying on a beach towel holding a book and laughing, do you? Never.

Thinking about it, I wasn't even sure I *wanted* people laughing out loud at my book. When I see someone cackling at a book I don't think, 'I've got to get a copy of that.' I think, 'I've got to get the hell away from this annoying person.'

Two lousy sentences. A stare-down contest ensued. Finally, I turned the computer off and studied the bump on my forehead in the screen's reflection. It occurred to me I was probably concussed. I felt strangely disassociated from the events of the day, as if they had all happened to someone else. What was really rattling me was the Rich Hall thing.

Outside, the storm gained intensity, charging the very foundations of the frail little house. I was in an increasingly agitated state, and I had to do something about it.

Mark Bolton, a man devoid of small pleasantries, answered his front door. He was wearing a frayed cardigan, a pair of magnifying specs perched atop his head. He looked me up and down and said, 'You're back early. Come on in.'

I stepped into the living room and kicked the snow off my boots. The house was cramped but comfortable. Copies of *The Livingston Enterprise* were strewn about. A child's safety seat sat on coffee table. An ice hockey match played soundlessly on the TV. Two short-haired pointers languished on a blanket-covered sofa. I seized on these small signs of domestication and wondered if Karen was home in London yet.

'Where's Carol?' I asked. Carol was Mark's wife, a transplanted Iowan.

'Asleep in bed with the kid. I'm making myself a Jack and Coke. You want one?'

'Sure.'

Crossing the living room, I reached down and patted one of the pointers on the head. They both shot off the couch in a frenzy, tore across the room and stood at attention by the front door.

'Nice one,' said Mark. 'You just gave them the signal to hunt.'

I followed him into the kitchen. There was a small breakfast nook next to the window. On the table sat a gooseneck lamp and an old Thompson 'A' vice. Bits of feather, marabou and hide were scattered about. The nook smelled of camphor and beeswax and brought to mind a different season – a season when the trout would be leaping and *Things Snowball* would be flying off bookshelves everywhere. In Montana, we spend the winter imagining the spring.

Mark went to a pie safe and pulled down a bottle of Jim Beam and two glasses. I sat down.

'I met your friend Rich Hall,' I said.

'Yeah? Helluva nice guy.'

'That's interesting that you would point that out.'

'What's that?'

'That he's a helluva nice guy.'

'What, you don't think so? Don't tell me he trashed your place. I vouched for him.'

'No. It's in perfect order.'

He went to the fridge and footed it open. His head disappeared inside, then he re-emerged with a can of Pepsi wedged under his chin.

I said, 'It's not unusual to be a helluva nice guy. What *is* unusual is that your guy just happened to be named Rich Hall.'

He shrugged and set the glasses down, poured out the Pepsi in twin measures.

'You don't find that remarkable?' I asked.

'I don't find it significant. It's just a name.' He splashed some Jim Beam. 'You writer types – you can't tell your little stories without throwing in a half-dozen *just happens*. The guy on the way to the airport *just happens* to have a flat tire and misses the plane that *just happens* to crash. Whaddya call that?'

'Coincidence.'

'Well, I call it horseshit – totally manufactured horseshit. That's why I've never finished a novel in my life. I'd rather fish.'

This was actually the thing I liked most about Mark: his primordial grounding, irritating though it could be. Everybody needs someone like him in their lives. When society eventually breaks down to savagery and rampant cannibalism, he's the guy who will keep you from getting eaten.

He slid a glass toward me. 'Where'd you get that ugly welt on your head?'

'I walked into a plate glass window.'

'I'll bet you're over there right now trying to turn that into one of your little stories.'

'As a matter of fact, I am.'

'I imagine it will contain a number of your little *coincidences*.' He almost spat the word out. 'What's the story about?'

I told him the scenario I'd dreamt up on the floor of the Hudson.

'So it's a sports-themed piece?'

'Uh, yes. I suppose.'

'Are you an expert on boxing? Wait, I can answer that for you. *No*. Why should anyone care what you have to say?'

'Because it's funny . . .'

'Funny to who?'

'*Whom* . . .'

'You're in Montana. *Who*?'

'I don't know. Boxing fans? People with a nostalgia for the days when boxing was about what happened inside the ring and not all the hoopla surrounding it. Come to think of it, why is it called a ring when it's clearly a square? See there, spatial relationships go right out the window the minute you get punched in the head.' *Note to self: Write that down. Something about, 'Don't tell me boxing doesn't cause brain damage . . .'*

He stared at me blankly.

'Mark, do you even own a sense of humor?'

'Not since Morecambe and Wise died.' Mark was a Lancastrian, originally from Great Harwood. But he'd been in Montana so long most of the British northerness had washed out, save for an occasional vowel that seemed to get trapped in his throat and roll around in there for a while searching for the exit. Most locals assumed he was a Minnesotan.

'Let me see if I've got this straight,' he said. 'You walk into a plate glass window and *just happen* to see a photo of Mike Tyson. Then the WBO *just happens* to hear about it, and Roy Jones Jr *just happens* to need a fight . . . How many stop signs did you run through there?'

'Humor allows its reader to suspend a certain amount of disbelief!'

'Why?'

'As a reward for their efforts.'

'Horseshit. Every one of those events is manipulated.'

He flipped his magnifiers down, reached into his fly box, pulled out two tiny feathers, paired them to a hook, then pulled the thread until they stood up in a hackle. He tightened the hook's shank to the vice jaws. Then, with a surgical flourish of the thread, created a reasonable imitation of a fly. He removed it and held it to the lamp for inspection.

'Now here's a story,' he said. 'I once watched an osprey pluck a trout

out of the Shields River and soar away with it. Just sail off into the blue forever. Forty minutes later, I'm driving by that telecom tower on Old Clyde Park Road – the one across from the auto graveyard. I *just happen* to look up and what do I see but the same osprey, sitting in its nest, with the fish in its mouth. Feeding its babies. Coincidence?'

'Absolutely.'

'No. Natural occurrence. A phenomenally pure experience. Now I didn't have to manufacture that story, did I? It *happened*. And, as far as I know, that osprey doesn't answer to a fucking *name*.'

I thought about this for a moment.

'You're making bugs,' I said.

'So?'

'You're making fake bugs to trick an innocent creature. Would you not call that manipulation?'

He stared at me. 'I'm making bugs because I gotta fish. And I gotta fish to feed the hungry little mouth asleep in the next room. You don't get that?'

'Of course . . .'

'No, I don't think you do. I shot about 250 million sperm into my wife's blameless uterus and one – *one!* – made it through. Picture those odds.'

'I don't think I want to.'

'Of course you don't because they're astronomical. Beyond human comprehension. Yet, it *just happens*, doesn't it? *Just happens*, every minute of the day in every fucking corner of the world, another halfloid-diploid squirts into existence. Let me tell you something.' He dabbed the fly into a small bowl of lacquer, then set it down to dry. 'Once you've got a kid, *coincidence* doesn't mean shit. Only the natural world makes sense. Put that in your book.'

Struggling back to my place, I got hit by a gust so violently, it spun me in my tracks. I was wearing cowboy boots – completely inappropriate for polar conditions – and the blast just kind of skated me up the street. I got my elbows out just in time to keep from face-planting. When I looked up, a deer was staring at me, eyes like titanium.

'Hello,' I said.

He stood, forelegs splayed, trying to fathom the underdressed idiot in a blizzard. Then, a terrifying roar. Out of the whiteness the headlights of a county snowplow appeared, bearing down on me, grinding up snow and razors of ice – my tax dollars at work. The deer shot off in a blur. I tried to scramble to my feet, but I was like a spaniel on linoleum. At the last moment, I pitched myself sideways and slammed up against a bank of hard-packed snow just as the plow's blade churned by, missing my head by inches.

For the second time that day, I found myself staring heavenward. I thought about what Mark had said. That he played at ignorance to keep his life uncomplicated was obvious. Yet he had rattled me, filled me with doubts. Not just about the boxing story, but the *entire* book – every manufactured chapter. How many stop signs *had* I run? Good writing, like good comedy, is supposed to arrive at some small truth. But, Lord, how much contrivance does it take to get there?

I lay there for a long time. The Jim Beam I'd consumed gave me a warm interior glow, and I seemed to think more lucidly on my back. It occurred to me in the face of all these near-death experiences – concussion, airplane near-crash, Emmy attack, killer snowplow – maybe this wasn't the day to be attempting whimsy.

'Much like Sugar Ray Leonard's retina, I am fairly detached,' I said out loud. The words came out in comic book clouds of frozen breath. No longer funny – if they ever were in the first place. In a blizzard, no one can hear you laugh.

'Humor books!' I called out. 'Bastard misfits of the publishing world! Misshapen, random, jumbled, witless drivel, jockeying for attention. Psssst! Over here. I'm the *Big Book of Fart Jokes*. I'm on the same shelf as Stephen Fry!'

I licked snowflakes off my lips and ran through a mental checklist of the influences that had acted upon me and driven me to be a comedian, trying to define myself by implication: my discordant parents, my love of reading, my most unreasonable dreams, a need to prove myself, a desperate desire to make a mark in the world while still being allowed to sleep till noon. *I am a professional liar*, I thought to myself. That's what I do. From that very first moment back in the seventies when I'd donned a white linen suit and tried to pass myself off as an evangelist, my livelihood, my credit rating, my Emmy, my writing, my current languor revealed but one road back to the light of day and that road was paved with professional lies. Thank God for Karen, who conditioned things, who allowed me to emerge as an occasional actual human being. She alternated between seeing into me and seeing right through me. Of course, for a liar like me, such truth filled me with dread.

Once back inside my house, I picked up the phone and called her in London.

'How was the flight?'

'I just got in. You okay?'

'I'm in Montana.'

'That's nice for you.'

'No, it's not. I think I've lost my sense of humor. Tell me if this is funny: I walked into a plate glass partition, and it knocked me down, but it didn't knock me out. Given the anemic state of boxing in the last few years, I am now scheduled to fight Roy Jones Jr in July.'

Silence.

'Hello? Anything?'

'Have you been drinking?'

'I walked into plate glass. It has the same effect.'

'Have you seen a doctor?'

'I'm snowed in! Among a raft of other calamities. The plane nearly crash-landed in Bozeman. And a guy, get this, a guy named Rich Hall—'

'*Rich Hall?*'

'I don't know, some friend of Mark's, was staying at my place—'

'*Why?*'

'—and when I climbed in through the window, he tried to brain me with my Emmy. There was an incident with a snowplow. And, to top it all off, I'm 2,000 words short on my book.'

A long silence as I waited for her to absorb all this. Then she said, 'Write that.'

'What?'

'The story of the extraordinary lengths you'll go to to avoid writing.'

'You make it sound like I willed these things to happen.'

'Subconsciously, you probably did. I know you. You're Mr Avoidance.'

'I'm not avoiding anything. I'm *trying to* write.'

'Are you? Then why are you on the phone with *me?* For goodness sakes, stop brooding and microfocus. *Finish the damn book.* Turn off your computer and try writing longhand. Feel the words flowing through you.'

I listened without listening. It was good just to hear her voice, pitiless but sensible. It melted the tone of the impending apocalypse. I rested my head on the desktop and sighed, shriven by separation: night and day. Five thousand miles. An ocean.

'So, do you think the boxing idea is funny?' I said.

'Funniest thing I've ever heard in my life at 6.39am. I'm going back to bed. Get your head out of your arse. Bye.'

I turned off all the lights, lit the new red candle and abandoned myself to objectless composition, my pen making vigorous shadows across a yellow legal pad. It felt primitive and industrious, and Karen once again had been right.

I stuck with my original boxing idea. To process all the real misfortunes of the day into a believable story – and not just a string of coincidences – was too daunting. That was for a future time and a better book. Right now, the task was to finish *Things Snowball*.

I wrote. Without inspiration or value. Driven by nothing more than contractual obligation. Like a boxer just trying to finish the last round, hoping he's ahead on points.

Currently my situation stands as follows: I will fight Roy Jones Jr in July, provided I can settle my dispute with the WBO-WBC-IBF-Fight News supercluster, which doesn't recognize my standing and claims to have never heard of me . . . and providing Dariusz Michalczewski agrees to fight Bosnian boxer Felix Sturm, or the actual country of Bosnia itself . . . and providing Bosnia agrees not to fight Serbia . . .

When I read it back, it actually didn't look half-bad. What it lacked in humor it made up for in teeth. *A think-piece*, I told myself. *Read it and scratch your whiskers and go, 'Hmmmm . . .'*

I finished the longhand version, spent another hour transcribing it on the computer, spellchecked it and, at precisely 9.45am London time, hit the send button. I yelled, *'Done!'* – only because I imagined it's something authors probably do. I briefly contemplated rewarding myself with a cigarette, like James Caan in *Misery*, but decided against it and went into the kitchen and poured myself a generous whiskey. I raised an empty toast and emulated celebration. *I have a book coming out in the spring! Is it funny? Who knows? Is it a pointless act of defiance to a long-departed dad? Absolutely! Does that make you feel better? Yes. Maybe. No.*

The wind tearing at the kitchen window sounded like a stadium cheer. I knocked down the whiskey in one draw and poured another.

I was on my third when the phone rang.

Surely it was my publisher, calling to congratulate me. I took my time walking into the dining room to answer because I was savoring the succession of images playing in my head: in a vast room, the rollers of a great offset press whirr into action. Pages, the ink still glistening, riffle into a collating tray. A man on a forklift piled high with newly bound books removes his hardhat, wipes his brow and tells his supervisor he desperately needs 'more *Things Snowball* floor space'. A warehouse worker leans against a wall, wets his finger, turns another page of *Things Snowball* and scans the room furtively. He knows he's supposed to get back to work, but he can't put the damn thing down.

It was Mark.

'Go to channel 105 on your TV.'

'Say what again?'

'Channel 105. On the TV.'

I tucked the phone under my chin, went into the living room and fumbled around in the dark for the remote.

'What's all this about?' I asked.

'I was flipping through the channels, trying to get the kid back to sleep, and look what came up.'

I finally located the remote, sensibly placed on a shelf above the TV, and silently cursed Rich Hall for his efficiency. I scrolled through the program guide and found 105: *Classic Boxing*. One of those obscure channels at the ass-end of the cable spectrum.

'It's your man, Roy Jones Jr,' Mark said.

Indeed, it was. I didn't recognize the opponent, but whoever he was, ol' Roy was going to town on him. The opponent's wild eyes darted around the ring as if he knew there was no escape. Roy caught him with an uppercut so vicious, I felt my own legs wobble.

'Ouch. Who's he fighting?' I asked.

In a remarkably flat tone, Mark said, 'Richard Hall. Jamaican fella.'

I sat down lifelessly on the sofa and took a deep breath, chalking the day up to forces beyond my control. 'There goes my story,' I said.

'What's that?'

'The idea of Rich Hall fighting Roy Jones Jr.'

'Oh yeah. I suppose you're right. Could be some legal issues, huh?'

'Yeah. The law of probability.' I hung up.

I sat there and watched the fight, trying to register a resigned detachment. Outside, the storm showed no signs of letting up. Jones Jr worked Richard Hall into the corner, pummeling him with pneumatic precision. Finally, the referee stepped in, arms a-flail, and halted the bloodbath. A commentator, in the timbre of an over-excited coroner, pronounced, 'Richard Hall is finished.'

'Except,' I said, 'I'm not.'

CHAPTER 6

WALKING THE ROOM

In April of 2006, I bought a ranch: 121 acres, up in the Shields Valley of Montana. My friend, the cowboy realtor Dave Viers, drove me out to see it. The place had never even gone on the market. Its previous owner had ceased making mortgage payments, filed a 'quit claim' and headed for the Bakken oil fields in North Dakota.

The house itself wasn't much to write home about. 'A piss and a look-around,' Dave called it. But, oh, the look-around! Three mountain ranges. A creek gurgling through the middle of the property. Antelope grazing at the fence-line. A sturdy log barn – Swedish joinery, gambrel roof, three working stalls and a corral. I stood under the imperial blue of a Western sky and had what you might call a *satori*. I saw myself leading Dixie, our thirteen-month-old daughter, around the breaking pen on a spotted grulla pony. Karen hanging laundry out on the line, clothes-pins in her teeth, her cotton print dress fluttering in the soft mountain breeze. Car wheels on a gravel road. Distant neighbors come a Sunday callin' to sample Karen's prepared-from-scratch Scouse stew and marvel at her funny accent. Dixie would learn to lope, rope and dally, eventually be crowned Miss Rodeo Montana – or, at the very least, runner-up – leave home and join the professional barrel-racing circuit. Karen and I would get old together on the porch. See the tree, how big it's grown.

We still had our little place on Clark Street in Livingston – the two-bedroom timber-frame – but it seemed to be shrinking day by day. I had a picture in my head of driving Karen and Dixie up into the Shields Valley, through the cottonwoods, over the crest, under the big wooden header, across the cattle guard, up the gravel road and just, well, springing it on her: 'It's a beautiful spot, honey, but *you'll* make it a beautiful home.'

Needless to say, I may have acted a bit rashly.

I closed the deal in Dave's office that afternoon. Dave wore a wide-brimmed Stetson with an old-fashioned Gus crease. A pair of auburn-handled Wild Bill Hickok Colt .22s was mounted in a Plexiglas case on the wall behind his desk – strictly for collectible purposes, not a sales tool.

'Why'd the ranch owner stop making payments?' I asked.

'I guess the ranching life's not for everyone. Which brings me to a question: you tell Karen you're doing this?'

'No. It's a surprise.'

'Like I just said, it's not for everyone.'

'We've *talked* about it.'

'Liar.'

'I once said, "Karen, what do you think of living on a ranch?" She said she liked the idea.'

'I've been through three wives who liked the *idea* of living on a ranch. Look, I'm as unscrupulous as any other realtor out there, but I cannot in good conscience sell you this place without your wife knowing about it.'

'She'll procrastinate, Dave. She'll hem and haw. She'll want to see a dozen other places.'

'That's what I'm here for.'

'And in the end, she won't make up her mind. She'll *agonize*. I'll *antagonize*. Finally, she'll throw up her hands and say, "For God's sake, buy the damn thing if it makes you happy." Long story short, my wife wants me to be happy, Dave. Sell me the ranch.'

Dave pursed his lips together and blew a very un-cowboy-like saliva bubble. Then he went to a file cabinet, gathered the paperwork and put it in front of me.

'What am I signing?'

'Grantee deed. Purchase contract. Water rights. Maybe your own divorce papers.'

The very next day I flew to Las Vegas to start a six-night run at the Riviera Hotel and Casino Comedy Club. Karen and Dixie were flying in from London to meet me. My plan was to finish out the week, then we would all head up to Montana.

The Riviera put me up in a suite in one of its 'luxury towers'. An hour before I was due onstage, Karen wheeled a stroller across the threshold and announced, 'It walks!'

I looked down at Dixie, blissfully asleep.

'Took her first steps on the plane,' Karen said. 'The two guys sitting across from us bought me champagne.' She assessed the room. 'They call this a *suite*? We could do with more space.'

You're about to see more space than you ever imagined, I thought.

A uniformed valet showed up and muscled Karen's luggage into the room. I tipped him ten bucks, then sat on the bed and admired my daughter while Karen showered and changed. She wanted to see the casino. I'd booked a babysitter from an agency listed in the *Las Vegas Visitors' Guide*: Granny Helpers. They claimed they could be 'in your room in twenty minutes', which was astonishing. *I* couldn't get to my own room in twenty minutes. The slot machines made me dizzy. The carpeting made me seasick. I could never discern which tower I was staying in, or which corridor led to it. These Granny Helpers must have the instincts of a homing pigeon.

Granny arrived in the form of a nineteen-year-old brunette wearing a tight plaid skirt. Karen pulled me into the bathroom. She was pretty certain the girl was a hooker moonlighting as a babysitter. I said I thought she was probably a college student.

'Well, she's certainly not a grandmother.'

'It's Vegas. Anything is possible.'

Karen went back in the bedroom and talked the girl through the usual precautions. 'Dixie will likely sleep the whole time,' she explained. 'You can catch up on your knitting.' It went right over the girl's head.

On the ride down in the elevator, Karen gave me the once-over. 'What's wrong?' she said.

'Nothing.'

'Something's up. What have you done?'

'Nothing!'

'What are you about to do?'

'*Nothing.* My show. I'm thinking about my show.'

I wasn't thinking about my show. I was thinking of a name for the ranch: *The Whistling Dixie.*

Downstairs, Karen went straight to the Splash Lounge, ordered a piña colada and spun around on her barstool like a five-year-old, looking wide-eyed at the crowds, the slots, the commotion. To me, a casino is what the inside of a migraine headache must look like. But I still got a kick out of seeing its impact on fresh visitors.

It took all of five minutes for Karen to discover something I'd never noticed: beneath each video poker console, at knee level, was a change-return slot for rejected quarters. Karen reached down and found one.

'Well now,' I said, 'you're playing with the house's money.' Little did I know how quickly this small turn of luck would coalesce into discomfiting urgency.

She inserted the quarter, and it shot straight to the reject slot again. Anybody else would have left it at that. Karen called the barman over. 'Excuse me, what's your name?'

'Adam.'

'Adam, I'm wondering if I can exchange this twenty-five-cent piece for another?'

He looked at me. I held my palms up as if to say, 'I have never seen this woman before in my life.' Adam went to the cash register and returned with a new quarter, polishing it sarcastically with his bar towel, and presented it to her like a precious gem. I knew I was going to have to tip him an extra dollar for this little benefaction.

Karen drew four tens and her fingers tap-danced across the hold buttons.

'Where did you—'

'They taught me on the plane,' she explained.

'*They*? Would that be the same guys who plied you with the champagne?'

The machine gave her eight credits. Then she drew a full house, followed by another combo. In no time she was up eighty credits. I walked her over to the cashier's window, and she came away with a crisp twenty-dollar bill, beside herself with glee. She found a roulette table, clapped her hands together and rubbed them briskly, as though she had a pleasant surprise in store for the other players.

'Who wants to watch the blonde win?' she called out. She put the twenty on red and doubled it. Then red again. Then black. I watched the pile of wheel chips expanding in front of her and put my hand on her back to indicate maybe it was time to cash in.

'What?'

'You're pushing your luck, honey.'

'I've got plenty of luck left. What I could use is another piña colada.'

She barely acknowledged me when I returned with the drink and told her I had to go, that my show was starting upstairs. 'Break a leg, hubs,' she mumbled, never taking her eyes off the wheel. It clattered to a satisfying stop, and the croupier pushed another stack at her. I turned to leave.

'Now I would like to make a snake bet,' I distinctly heard her say.

'I don't understand these idiots who drive Winnebagos,' I remarked from the stage. 'Why spend like a millionaire to live like the homeless?'

It was just a throwaway line, but the entire crowd reacted like they'd been slapped in the face. No one had told me the casino was hosting an RV-owners convention. Polyester attire and the smell of VapoRub should have been a heads-up, but I wasn't focused. After all, my wife was downstairs exhibiting Sharon-Stone-in-*Casino* tendencies. My daughter was being babysat by a potential hooker. I was an undisclosed rancher. My head wasn't in this game.

'Oh, I'm sorry. Did I offend you people? If anyone in this room owns a recreational vehicle, you have every right to get up, walk out to the parking lot, start up your home in complete disgust and drive away.'

An older couple near the front made a big dramatic display of heading for the exit. The husband couldn't have been over five-foot-five.

'I think you'll find you don't have many friends in this room,' he broadcast, jabbing a finger into his wife's spine to prod her along.

'Call us when you get there, Mr and Mrs Old-and-In-the-Way,' I replied. 'You know how we worry!' I could hear them slam the showroom door on the way out. 'How does that little fella even see over the dashboard?' I asked. 'He must navigate by tuning in to the local radio stations.'

More defections. In stand-up parlance, this is known as 'walking the room'. Now and then, you misjudge a crowd so badly that you just want to purge them and start afresh. It's highly unprofessional and oddly edifying.

I decided to play a little game with the crowd. I turned to a couple in matching gold-braided nautical caps at a front table.

'You, cap'n. What kind of land yacht do you drive?'

'What *kind*?'

'What make? Model. Winnebago? Odyssey? Sunseeker?'

'Diplomat.'

'Okay. You folks call out the makes and models of your mobile death-traps, and I'll put the word *anal* in front of it. Let's see who comes up with the best porn title. "Anal Diplomat". Who can top that?'

A good portion of the crowd did not share my enthusiasm and voted with their feet. For the diehards who stayed, the best we came up with were 'Anal Windjammer', 'Anal Pioneer' and 'Anal Family Jamboree'.

When I got back to our room, Karen was in bed and Dixie was in her onesie, teetering unsteadily against the floor-to-ceiling window, her fingers splayed like a tree frog. I joined her for the view.

Our suite looked westward, but not in the historical sense. You could see McCarran Airport, which gave way to the freeway, which gave way to the seething tumult of California. I was more partial to any other aspect, where the neon ended abruptly at the edge of True West: Nevada, Utah, Idaho and, eventually, Montana.

'What would you say to your own horse?' I whispered to Dixie.

'*Horse*,' Dixie replied.

Karen roused and switched on the bedside lamp.

'You're awake,' I said.

'How can I sleep? I'm up $1,200.' Her use of the word *up* suggested an ongoing venture. She found the remote and turned on the TV: Conan O'Brien hyperventilating with the house band. Conan's guest, an actor I didn't recognize, watched this exchange cautiously, not getting the jokes. *That* resonated.

'What's this about a horse?' Karen asked.

'Oh nothing. Just—'

'Where in God's name would we keep a horse?'

I changed the subject. 'I'm pretty sure I'm in trouble.'

She switched off the TV. 'What did you do?'

'Walked a roomful of RV owners.'

'RV . . . what?'

'Caravans, you'd call them.'

'Do they still take you out to the desert and make you dig your own grave?'

'No. They just replace you with a new comic.'

'So, now what?'

'We can fly up to Montana early.'

'I wanted to see the outlet malls.'

'Fine. We can stick around for a day.' *You'll look, but you won't buy anything.*

'And the Forum Shops at Caesar's. I've got money to burn.'

'Okay. Dixie and I can have a desert adventure.' *Dixie, you and*

189

I are going to the Boot Barn. Daddy's gonna buy you a little cowgirl outfit – matching blue boots and straw hat. A little foreshadowing could be quite effective here.

'Horse,' Dixie replied, imagining all the possibilities.

Karen and the kid woke up early with fierce jet lag, so we all went down to the coffee shop for breakfast. Judging from the reactions of the diners, I'd miraculously acquired the power to make forkfuls of food hover midway between plate and mouth. Karen noticed it right away. We found a booth, and I took a seat facing the keno screen on the wall.

'What the hell did you *say* to these people last night?' she asked.

'It doesn't matter. Let's just eat and get out of here.'

Karen picked up a menu and began to study it like an essay. I made some patently transparent efforts at playing with Dixie in her highchair, thinking it might buy me back some humanity, but she spurned me for a bottle of Tabasco sauce. I ended up having to wrestle it – quite demonstratively – from her grasp, which, frankly, did nothing to absolve my pariah status among the diners. I could feel collective disgust burning the back of my neck. *Don't look, Earl, but the degenerate comedian who soiled our evening is actually a father! Call social services.*

A waitress appeared at our table and tapped her foot impassively. Hard wrinkles radiated from the edges of her eyes and mouth: a real desert face. 'Your little girl is entitled to all the free breakfast she wants till 9am,' she explained, as if somehow this might speed things up.

'Could you give us a few minutes?' Karen asked brusquely. Hearing a British accent, the waitress made a noise that sounded like *ee-yuh* and walked away.

'What's her problem?'

'This town doesn't warm to British visitors.'

'Why?'

'It runs on palm grease. You Brits have dry hands.'

Right then – as if I didn't have enough attention already – I heard my name being paged over the public address system. I had to walk back through the restaurant and its lingering disgrace to get to a paging phone. Diners recoiled. Whatever it was I had, they didn't want to catch. When I returned, Karen had finally settled on Eggs Florentine.

'The Director of Entertainment wants to see me right away,' I said. 'You should probably go upstairs and pack.'

'Jim Button and I have been discussing how to handle your situation,' said Gerald Bussman, the recently appointed Interim Entertainment Director for Riviera Enterprises. He was explicitly avoiding eye contact with me. He wore a cobalt-blue jacket with a glittery shawl collar that one could possibly get away with if one wasn't named Gerald Bussman. 'I think you have a pretty good idea how *I'd* deal with it. But this man sitting across from me is vice president of . . . what is it again, Jim?'

'NRVOA,' Jim Button said, an affable-enough looking fellow. 'National Recreational Vehicle Owners Association.'

'Right. Jim has a unique proposal. Sit down. Hear him out.'

I crossed the room to shake Jim's hand, but he waved me off, and I realized the affability was just a front. I took a seat next to him, facing Gerald and his scary jacket.

'Evidently, you're not a fan of RV owners,' Jim Button said. 'Might I ask why?'

I turned in my chair and looked him right in the eye. I didn't care for this guy, nor did I care any longer for Las Vegas. I just wanted to retreat with my family to Montana. I said, 'I believe they are the descendants of barbarians. Hoarders with no place to hoard. So, they take to the highways with their boats, motorbikes, canoes, barbeque grills, lawn furniture – everything they own – strapped to the side of what is, for all intents, a motorized toilet. It's crass. Vulgar. A perversion of the American frontier spirit and all it ever stood for. You want me to go on?'

A pause, then Gerald asked, 'One of 'em run over your dog or something?'

Jim Button was looking up at a corner of the ceiling, where there was nothing to see. His gaze came swooping down on me like a vulture. 'How'd you like to take a little drive out to the desert?'

I suddenly felt queasy. It was my belief this nostalgic form of Vegas retribution had long passed.

Jim reached into his coat pocket. He pulled out a set of keys on a black fob. 'You'll find it in guest parking.'

'*What?*'

'A thirty-five-foot Winnebago Adventurer. Fully loaded. Fully insured. Yours to drive for six months!'

'This is a joke, right?'

'Far from it, Mr Hall. I can say that with dead certainty. I'd like to change your attitude.' He dropped the keys on the desk and slid them in front of me. 'What would you say, as a comedian, is your biggest performance *asset*?'

'I don't understand that question . . .'

'I'll tell you: it's your audience. People. They see you onstage, television. They tell their friends, "I saw the funniest guy last night." "Oh, really? What did he *talk* about?" "He *talked* about this wonderful RV trip he took with his family."'

'*Ahh* . . . You want me to be some sort of lifestyle ambassador.'

Jim feigned deference. 'I can't tell you what to do, Mr Hall. But I feel assured – and I believe a raft of aggressive libel law experts will back me up on this – once you get behind the wheel of that motorhome and out on the open road, you won't hesitate to *share* the exhilaration with your . . . followers.'

I looked to Gerald. 'Can't you just fire me?'

He didn't look at me but rather observed the tip of his finger trailing along the length of his desk, as if charting the progress of a bug. 'I think Jim's made you a sensible offer,' he said. 'And tonight, when you go up onstage and *apologize wholeheartedly* for embarrassing this casino and it's cherished guests—'

'And announce your conversion—' Jim piped in.

'Some thoroughly decent people will find it in their hearts to put this incident behind them.' Gerald's eyes finally met mine. 'I know I will.'

Jim Button leaned forward, picked up the keys again and jiggled them in front of my face, grinning like a sadistic jailer.

*

'This is bigger than our house,' Karen marveled. We were standing inside the monstrosity: a spaceship built to transport a colony of simpletons to a color-blind planet. The predominant décor scheme was rustic vomit. Everything about it – right down to the smell – was synthetic: vinyl, plastic, formaldehyde. Karen was enthralled.

'I don't understand. They just *gave* this to you?'

'For six months.'

'Why?'

'I'm not quite sure. In this town, revenge and reward are virtually indistinguishable from each other. It's Vegas voodoo. But I'll tell you this much, we're not going *anywhere* in this contraption.'

'Might be fun,' she said. She plopped Dixie into the Euro Chair, pushed its footrest, and the recliner swept back, leaving Dixie to gaze wondrously at the ceiling. I watched, alarmed, as my wife scuttled over to the dinette, squeezed in and mimed eating an imaginary dinner. Then she was up again, running a verbal checklist of mod-cons: 'Big-screen TV, convection microwave . . . oh my *gawd*, look at all these cabinets!' For some reason, she'd affected a beautician's rasp, possibly meant as sarcasm. 'A girl could get used to this!' she cried and drifted out of view into the rear master bedroom.

I climbed in the driver's seat and stared through a Cinerama-sized windscreen at the hundreds of other RVs in the Riviera parking lot: an occluded, thoroughly disturbing vista. I put my hands to the steering wheel. It was like a Ferris wheel. The entire rig was not only an abomination, but it was an *ill-timed* abomination – one that threatened to undercut my own elaborate surprise.

Karen returned, lifted Dixie in her arms and sat down. 'Everything about this is hideous,' she said. She stretched her legs out and swiveled around like a CEO. 'But I love it.'

This was infinitely depressing, and she read it in my face.

'What's wrong?' she said.

'I'll tell you,' I answered, and I almost did. 'I'm perfectly capable of accommodating my own family.'

'What an odd thing to say.' She considered this for a moment. 'Do you feel emasculated?'

'No.' Then I *did* tell her. 'I've bought a ranch.'

'You what?'

'I bought a ranch. For us. Up in the Shields Valley.' It got loudly, loudly quiet. These Winnebagos, I noticed, were well insulated for sound. 'I was going to surprise you. But now seems like a pretty good time to mention it.'

'A better time to mention it would have been *before* you bought it.'

'It came up really quickly, hon. I had to move fast—'

'Caught up in the moment, were you? I can only imagine. You looked out over a majestic sweep of land and felt the confluence of time calling . . .'

'Whoa, now . . .'

'Come, Rich, let us bridge the mythic Western past with all that is yet to be,' she said sarcastically. 'I think I'm going to be ill. How many bathrooms?'

'Three. One en suite. Look, I'll finish out the week, then we'll just head on up there and look at it.'

'Just *mosey* on up to the spread . . .'

'If you don't like it, I can flip it really fast. It's a very desirable location.'

'That's not really the point though, is it?' She shifted Dixie to her other knee and stared out into the parking lot. 'Well, right then. This is turning into quite an eventful little trip. I believe I'll go visit some shops now.'

'Want me to come with you?'

'No. I prefer shopping on my own.' She lifted Dixie up and dropped her in my lap. 'Much like you.'

Jim Button was right. My attitude did change. Especially after I bought some three-foot-high magnetic letters, which spelled out RICH HALL, and slapped them on both sides of the Winnebago. I spent the afternoons cruising around Vegas. Tourists and passers-by craned their necks and nudged their companions, taking credit for a discovery that wasn't theirs.

There goes Rich Hall!

Who's Rich Hall?

Hell if I know. But he's got his own tour bus.

I didn't doubt that some people knew me. But I got a bigger kick out of making people think they *should* know me. There are two ways to become famous in showbiz – *head-turning* famous: work hard, put in your time, hone your craft and claw your way to the top. Or just get yourself a big fuck-off Winnebago and plaster your name to the side. That'll do the trick.

*

Karen adopted a kind of judicial mien, somewhere between terse and threatening. *Stroppy*, I believe the Brits call it. The mere mention of 'the Montana place' was like a dynamite fuse. At lunch one day, our server asked what kind of dressing I wanted on my salad. I told her ranch. Karen lowered her menu, glared at me and said, 'Know that Dixie and I are prepared to make other arrangements if you insist on acting out these cowboy fantasies of yours.'

'It's not a fantasy, hon. It's a home. Just try, please try, to trust my intentions. We'll work it out!' This all had the tonality of a man back-pedaling from a disaster. 'I'm thinking of calling it the *Whistling Dixie Ranch*.'

'I have a better name: *The Pinhead Ponderosa*.' Still, I could sense her guard dropping. It helped to have Dixie on my side, whose newfound ability to utter 'horse' at the slightest prompting helped soften Karen up. I loved that child with all my heart, particularly for her veto power.

Saturday night. Last show.

'Ladies and gentlemen, please welcome Rich Hall!'

Trepidatious applause. *The crowd's heard a few things about this guy.*

'How many RV owners in the room?' I asked.

A show of hands.

'My first night onstage here, I was a little hard on some of y'all.' Note the infusion of a little Southern gumbo to imply folksy solidarity. 'I'd never been behind the wheel of one of those things. But now I have. The fine people of the Winnebago Corporation of Forest City, Iowa, actually gave me one to drive – a thirty-five-foot Adventurer!'

Murmurs of awe from the crowd.

'And I have to say, it's a thing of wonder. I filled it up with fuel and a new country formed in the Middle East.'

Big laughter from the crowd.

'That's so true, they're gas guzzlers,' someone muttered, insipidly. It wasn't a truth. It was a total distortion of the truth. I'd been doing my best all week to placate these imbeciles.

'Now,' I said, 'I'm spending like a millionaire to live like the homeless!'

Applause. Same damn joke as the first night. But because I was now speaking *for* them and not *against* them, they bought every word of it. There might be a lesson in there for new comedians, I don't know.

I worked the crowd over for a good forty minutes, then decided to go for broke.

'Hey, let's play the RV game! Call out the make and model of your RV, and I'll put the word *anal* in front of it . . .'

Astoundingly, *no one* walked out. The winner was 'Anal Teardrop'.

Jim Button was waiting at the back of the showroom when I came offstage, his face the color of a radish. 'Give me the keys.'

'Hell no, Jim. You said six months.'

'The *keys* . . .'

'I'm driving that baby to Montana. You want it back, come get it.'

'What climate control setting do we prefer?' Karen asked, fiddling with the dashboard console. 'Springtime in the Laurentians? Malibu Eventide?'

It was encouraging to see she had her sense of humor back. Vegas was behind us. We were headed north up Nevada 93, ultimately to our shining foothills heaven on the northern Rockies range. Karen had adorned the RV with fairy lights and Fiestaware, rugs, throw cushions, a tea kettle, a biscuit tin, a plaster coiled rattlesnake ashtray that served no purpose whatsoever (no one smoked), a hand-made grandma quilt that covered the godawful 'power-couch', and a lightbox mounted over the cooker, showing a vintage Airstream parked in front of some pines above the words 'God Bless our Happy Camper'. Dixie was strapped snugly into the Euro Chair, immersed in *The Magic Roundabout* on the VCR-TV above her head.

If all this was meant to suggest domestic tranquility, it didn't. I was white-knuckled at the wheel and only marginally in control of my bearings. The Venturi effect of the high desert winds lifted and plummeted the vehicle at will, like a plane hitting turbulence. I couldn't keep the thing in the proper lane. Invariably, a car would materialize alongside us, its occupants rubbernecking for a glimpse of the superstar within. If they could have seen through the tinted windows, they would have witnessed a man silently mouthing the words 'still alive' much too ardently for anyone's comfort but his own.

By four that afternoon I was a wreck. I didn't think I could wrestle the Adventurer much further and suggested we get a motel room.

'Why would we do that?' said Karen. 'We're *in* a motel room.'

I was too frazzled to argue. South of Ely, Nevada, I stopped at a travel plaza to refuel. Karen went inside to call ahead for campground reservations. While the tank was filling, I walked around the RV and pulled my name down from the sides, no longer desiring to be famous.

Thirty minutes later, we pulled into the Ely RV Campground. I went into the office to register. An older couple – retirees, no doubt – ran the place with a kind of quasi-rural bonhomie that was, quite possibly, not genuine. The woman shoved a site map across the countertop at me.

'Congratulations. You're in a premium site with its own oasis. Pets?'

'We've stolen one of Siegfried and Roy's tigers.'

'Keep it leashed. Pull on through.'

We drove slowly through the campground with its lunatic geometry of vans, fifth wheels, pop-ups, travel trailers and toy haulers. Every one of them was tethered to a hook-up like a terminal patient. Barbeques, portable gennies, bug zappers, TV aerials, hammocks, kennels, paddling pools. There were people getting back to nature by throwing every possible convenience they could muster at its encroachment. They gazed in wonderment as our gleaming anodized *beast* trawled past – the Mother Ship arrived.

Our 'oasis' turned out to be a table-scrap of vegetation with a forlorn picnic table on it. Ten minutes later, I was trying to work out the RV's on-board levelling system when a face popped through the door, unannounced. 'Hey, neighbor! I come in?'

And just like that, he did – a stringy individual with a sleeve of tattoos. He had the kind of scabrous features that, for some reason, made me think of a Tasmanian Devil.

'Always wanted to see the inside of one of these!' he crowed. The view occasioned him to raise a can of Pabst Blue Ribbon to his mouth, close his eyes and savor a good portion of its contents. When he refocused, he seemed to notice me for the first time. His head shot back. 'Shit, friend! You're that comedian!'

'I am.'

'I was at your show last night!'

'Oh. Isn't that . . . something.'

'Honest to God, me 'n' the wife never laughed so hard in our lives. Hang on a sec, will ya? I gotta get her, I gotta introduce her to the comedian.' He shot out the door just as Karen appeared from the bedroom.

'Making friends already?'

'We need to keep that door locked.'

'I'm making a G&T,' she said. She made a little foxtrot move around me to get to the fridge. Stringy Guy reappeared in the doorway, this time with his wife peering over his shoulder – a piggy-eyed woman with a startling chignon, oft-attributed to cartoon librarians.

'Come on in,' I called tepidly. Introductions were dispensed all around. They were Tony and Lorraine – fugitives from justice, we would learn soon enough. I noted their T-shirts did not match but featured the same motif: a wolf howling at a full moon. I couldn't count the number of times I'd seen this theme throughout the past week, and I asked Tony if that was some kind of RV thing.

'Absolutely,' he said. 'We like to think of ourselves as a brotherhood of lone wolves.'

'That would constitute a *pack*,' Karen pointed out. Tony stared at her, opting not to follow that line of consideration.

Lorraine asked if she could see the rest of the RV. Karen extended a hand and told her, 'Be my guest. Careful not to wake the baby.' Lorraine bustled past.

'So, what's it like to be married to Mr Anal Adventurer, here?' Tony asked Karen, perhaps a tad too enterprisingly. 'He as funny in real life as he is onstage?'

'I'm sorry. *What* did you just say?'

Tony punched me on the arm. 'We have not stopped playing that game since we lit out from Vegas this morning.'

'What game?' said Karen, bewildered.

'You know, the anal RV game.'

'No, I don't know.'

I explained to Tony that Karen had not bothered to come to any of my shows during the week.

'Yeah, my wife's sick of all my jokes too,' Tony said. 'For the record, that's our "Anal Bigfoot" parked across from yours. Why don't you join us at suppertime? Lorraine's cooked up something wicked for tonight.'

'Would that be chili or meth?' Karen asked. I shot her a look. 'I'm going for a walk,' she announced and breezed out the door.

Later, when it was dark, Tony and I sat in his lawn chairs, roughly splitting the distance between our vehicles. He finished his umpteenth PBR and reached over his head.

'Look up there at the stars,' he said, waving in a vague direction. 'Any minute now, the crow, the cup and the water snake are gonna come into view.' I leaned back and searched the sky. I couldn't quite make out what he was pointing to.

'Right off the Big Dipper,' he indicated. His hand shot for the ice chest. 'Another beer, neighbor?'

'I'm fine, thanks.'

He was back to calling me *neighbor*. Throughout the evening, he'd kept forgetting my name. Then, when he would remember it again, overuse it. 'That's some rig you got there, Rich. I had an uncle named Rich. He was a farrier. Had a nice little set-up, but it washed away in a flood. How long you been a comedian, Rich?' That sort of thing.

Karen and Dixie were in bed. Lorraine had excused herself earlier, claiming she wanted to go inside and watch *The Tonight Show*. Moths, drawn to the blue flicker of the television, dive-bombed the screen-door of their Bigfoot travel trailer. A battered Silverado pick-up truck was parked next to it. Something about the newness of the trailer and that old truck didn't quite ally, but I let it pass.

'Where are you and Lorraine from?' I asked.

'Meeteetse, Wyoming, originally. I used to raise Tennessee Walkers. Lorraine was an equine vet. I guess it was kismet, how we met.'

'No, it wasn't. It was tequila shots!' came Lorraine's voice from inside their trailer. She must've been listening in.

'So, you two had a ranch?'

'We did, indeed. Seventeen years and no children. We both like kids, just didn't want to start our own brand. Which worked out, I suppose. Couldn't live this kind of life with a coupla sprogs in tow.'

'*This* kind of life?'

'Drifting. With a long view to the west.'

'What happened to the ranch?'

'The IRS was gonna get it. I filed a quit claim.'

'I've heard of those.'

'Best thing to do if you ain't bound by inheritance.'

'You don't miss it?'

'Ranching? Wouldn't wish it on my worst enemy.'

'Horses ain't nothing but Petri dishes with legs!' Lorraine called. 'Worms, lice, warbles, bowed tendons . . .'

'Broken fences, broken machinery . . .'

'Cracked hooves, lameness, wire cuts, ulcerated eyes, spavin, gravel founder and hay belly!'

'And, finally . . .' – Tony held up empty palms – 'just broke!'

This might have been funny if it hadn't been so over-rehearsed. Suddenly, I felt sober and awful. Sober in the realization of what I'd actually done: bought 121 acres of prime headache. Awful for what I was about to put Karen through. A ranch would be as foreign to her structured background as baseball, Waffle Houses or tipping. I accepted, right then, that I had made a colossal mistake. Not everyone wants to be a cowboy.

A low rumble caught Tony's attention and brought him forward in his chair. I looked over my shoulder and saw a car creeping through the campground with its lights off. Tony set his beer down carefully on the ground, continuing to talk, but absent from his own discourse.

'So anyway, Lorraine and me hit the road—'

'And the road hit back!': Lorraine.

'Yessir. Always got to have a plan B in life. *Plan B!* Right, Lorraine?'

'What's going on out there?' she called.

The car got closer and I could see it was a police cruiser.

'Just winding up the conversation, babe.' He stood up quickly. 'Do me a favor, will ya, neighbor? Anyone comes asking, you didn't see us.' Then he sprinted for the Silverado, Lorraine bounding out from the trailer to join him. They climbed in, started it up and peeled off in a ghostly cloud of getaway dust.

It took me a minute to fathom what I had just witnessed. Times, it seemed, had turned on the peerless dignity of the American rancher. The police car pulled up and, after a moment, its blue light came on. A patrolman climbed out, stood in the wedge of the open cruiser door and spoke into his radio. In the flashing light, I could see he was compact and disheveled, with a careless comb-over and a paunch. Not what you would call 'academy fresh'. He hung up the radio, pulled a Maglite from his holster, went over to the Bigfoot and knocked aggressively on the screen.

'Trouble, officer?' I called out.

Startled, he swung the Maglite around and trained it on my face. He came toward me. 'You staying here?'

'No, I'm staying *there*.' I shot my thumb toward the Winnebago.

He swung the flashlight beam past my head. 'You own it?'

'No, sir. It's on loan.'

'On *loan* . . .'

'From the National Recreational Vehicle Owners Association. Kind of an endorsement deal.'

He raked the beam across its width. Then he said, 'Who's Rich Hall?'

I turned. In the swath of light, my name was visibly outlined in road dust. 'That's me. I'm a comedian.'

He shot the light back on my face, blinding me. He was like a cinematographer with that damned thing. 'So, what . . . you *used* to be famous?'

'Yeah. Something like that.'

'You know the people staying in that trailer?'

'Never seen them. Can you turn that thing off?'

He switched the Maglite off and stood motionless in the dark. You could hear the hum of portable generators, the squawk of the police radio, cicadas, Jay Leno.

'You don't know them, but you're sitting on their furniture.'

'Yessir, I suppose I am.'

'I'm just waiting for you to say something I can sink my teeth into.'

'As you guys are so fond of saying, nothing to see here.'

'Was that one of your alleged jokes?'

'Not at all.'

I could feel him staring at me. Finally, he said, 'You run across the couple staying there, dial the sheriff's department.'

'I certainly will, officer,' I said. But I wasn't about to. I don't rat out my fans.

We pulled out the following morning. Karen, observing an X-slash of crime-scene tape on the door of the Bigfoot, decided we wouldn't eat breakfast till we were well out of White Pine County. I had sunk into complete apathy. The ranch had the feeling of receding, even as we were heading toward it. Dixie occupied herself with crayons and *Dora the Explorer*. Karen watched the road, studying every truck we passed. Somewhere out there were fugitives.

After Jackpot, Nevada, with its open-all-hours, last-chance

carnality, we crossed into Idaho – all potatoes and desolation. It was hard to tell where one ranch ended and another began. Karen stared out at the fortress-like compounds and asked, 'Who lives out here?'

'Mormons.'

'Everything looks defensive,' she said. She rolled down the window. The air smelled like potato chips.

By mid-afternoon, we picked up I-15, where a sumptuous span of passing lanes allowed me to relax a little. Then north to Whitehall, Montana, where the evergreens and vast cordilleras marked the end of recreation and the beginning of nature. Then I-90 East to Bozeman, over the pass and down the long descent into the Yellowstone River Valley. When we reached the spot on the river where I had proposed to her, I consciously slowed down, out of shared private reverence.

It had been on a June afternoon. We'd pulled our raft up onto a shoal by a splendid turn in the water. Minutes earlier, I'd passed under a golden eagle, staring down at us from the naked branch of an Engelmann spruce, which I took as a sign. I produced the ring from a waterproof storage bag while Karen unwrapped sandwiches.

'Let me think about it over lunch,' was her answer. She couldn't decide between the turkey 'n' Swiss or the ham 'n' cheddar. I was starving, and I wanted to spend the rest of my life with this woman, so I grabbed the turkey 'n' Swiss and tore into it.

'Let me make up your mind for you,' I said, with a mouth full of pulp. '"Yes, Rich, I will marry you."'

'Oh, alright then,' she answered. 'If it makes you happy.'

The Adventurer cleared the wooden header by an inch at best. In the middle of the gravel drive, under a sky the color of Gerald Bussman's jacket, a ferret and a badger were engaged in a standoff. The shadow of the advancing RV darkened over them, and they retreated into separate corners. I parked at the top of the hill and cut the engine. Karen stared up at the house.

In the ensuing dreadful silence, I took inventory of some notable shortcomings. The chimney cladding, for example, had collapsed. Paint was peeling off the deck. Some of the fences were broken.

Karen never said a word. Just climbed out, walked slowly toward the house and disappeared through the front door.

I carried Dixie down to the barn. The previous owner had hung a homemade swing from the rafters. I set her on it, squeezed her hands tight to the ropes, and pushed her gently back and forth. I pointed to the corrals and told her that's where horses lived.

'Horses,' she repeated. (Someday, when she reads this story, I hope she forgives me for some criminally underwritten dialogue.)

When I looked up, Karen was leaning against the side of the barn's big doorway, framed by the Crazy Mountains in the distance.

'If it's all the same to you,' she said, 'I'd prefer to stay in the house on Clark Street.'

'Okay.'

'Until we're done with the renovations.'

CHAPTER 7

BUNDY

I'd invented a character named Otis Lee Crenshaw. Confederate bandana, tattoos, soul patch, Southern drawl. Backed by a louche trio of marginally competent country musicians, he slouched behind an electric piano and growled wistful love ballads about prison rape and bag lady sex. It makes perfect sense that an ensemble of such caliber would be invited to tour Australia. This was in April of 2009.

One night, a few weeks into the run, I was sitting in an Adelaide dressing room nursing a beer and wondering, inspirationally, how much Otis had left in the tank. It was getting harder and harder to run the complicated guise of a six-times divorced, recidivist Tennessee convict – most recently paroled on blatantly trumped-up charges of endangered coral possession – through the needle eye of three-chord country music. I had a lot of unfinished songs: melodies that needed lyrics, premises that started out strong and fizzled, bread but no sandwich and the wrong kind of mustard.

There was a loud thump at the door and a young couple burst in, uninvited. The girl – mid-twentyish, dirty-blonde, maybe a dental appointment away from being gorgeous – slugged back a shot of rum straight from the bottle, mussed her hair into disarray and shrieked. 'Shittin' place is driving me nuts, Otis Lee Crenshaw! You out every night with your music mates and me expectin' a child!'

'Say what?'

'*What* my arse. You're hangin' out with poofters while I'm home with a torpedo in the tube!'

'How do you know the baby's mine, you splay-legged, truckstop Jezebel?' I answered. (God knows why I chose to play along with this.)

The guy accompanying her was laughing so hard, he fell backward into a dressing room chair, spilling his drink all over his flannel trousers.

'Whoa, mate,' he said. 'That's me sis.' He was older, with great mutton-chop sideburns and short-cropped hair.

'You're right. Enough of this psychotherapy,' I said. 'This is a private dressing room.'

'And this is a private visit. We want you to come to our grandad's funeral.'

'I don't do funerals.'

Something homicidal flashed across the guy's face then just as quickly passed. He stuck out a big meaty hand. 'X. Short for Xavier.'

I reached out to shake, and he yanked me toward him. You could smell sweat, body-spray, rum and trouble coming off him. 'Know that we are in mourning and pissed as farts.'

I looked over at his sister.

'I'm Temple,' she said. X was squeezing my hand in a death grip. 'Let him go, X. You're hurtin' him.'

He grinned. 'Just makin' friends with Otis Lee Crenshaw. Does this hurt?'

'I'm gonna say it does.'

'But not by half what we're feelin' inside right now.'

Right then and there, I should have peeled off the fake goatee and confederate bandana, revealed that Otis wasn't real and they were investing their collective grief in a fictional character. But there were so many emotional cue balls flying back and forth, I couldn't quite bring myself to do it.

'Let up,' I ordered. X loosened his grip. I was thinking, *Where the hell is backstage security? This is a goddamn theater.*

Temple walked over and extended a finger to the snap button on my cowboy shirt.

'Edgar would have loved to meet you,' she said, her voice now low and faltering.

'Edgar?'

'Granddad. Said you were his favorite comedian. He bought us tickets to this show.'

'How old?'

'Seventy-seven.'

'Ah . . .'

'Topped himself,' said X. 'Unlovely fact.'

'Topped himself?'

'You deaf, mate? Dead. Reversed off a car park and landed four stories down in front of the Coles supermarket.'

'He didn't top himself. It was an accident,' said Temple.

'Well, I'm sorely aggrieved to hear that,' I said. It sounded like something a contrite Otis would say.

'Bollocks,' X said. 'Dead is dead.' He peered into his drink, surprised to see it was now empty. 'Whaddya reckon happens when you die? Long light? Cheery tunnel? Not likely.' Then he proceeded to give a strict account of the afterlife: heaven, purgatory and hell. It was particularly vivid and seemed to be modelled on various aspects of a backwater Adelaide suburb called Elizabeth. Hell, for instance, was the waste-disposal site on the outskirts of town, phosphoric and rat-infested. Purgatory was a multi-story car park above a supermarket with a strict three-hour parking limit. But heaven? Ah, heaven . . . You entered heaven without having to use a stinking lift that smelled of piss or pass by the open doors of screaming neighbors and their bloody *irrit* kids.

'And in heaven,' Temple concluded, 'you never run out of Bundy.' 'Bundy' being Bundaberg Rum, a primordial Aussie concoction of (I'm certain) jet fuel, molasses and turpentine.

She leaned in, tried to kiss me, missed, glided over to the dressing mirror and began singing an Otis Lee Crenshaw song:

'There's a full moon shinin' on a stainless toilet bowl
An eight by twelve room shrinks every time that I'm denied parole'

Here's the thing, though: she had a hell of a voice. Open-throated and confident. I was a little mesmerized watching her.

'*My cellmate beats me black and blue*
But in the dark it's true . . .'

She shot me a tilted smile and nodded, a signal to pick up the refrain. I sang:

'*He almost looks like you . . .*'

We traded lyrics and had ourselves a real Dolly Parton–Kenny Rogers moment. X slouched in his chair, observing us with the kind of sloe-eyed visage you'd associate with the recently raised dead.

'You oughta take her on the road with ya,' he said.

'Nice set of pipes,' I said to Temple.

'I know all your songs, Otis,' she replied. 'Come to the service.'

'When?'

'Tomorrow.'

'I don't know. I ain't much for dressin' up.'

'No one says you gotta dress up. It's Elizabeth. We're an informal bunch.'

'Let me think about it,' I said. I was thinking, *This is what Otis needs: immersion.*

X lifted himself, rather ungainly on the weight of his huge fore-arms, and struggled to get his bearings. 'Let's go, Temple. This piker doesn't give a rat's arse about our family.'

He reached for her arm to pull her across the room. She spun and decked him squarely in the pelvis, and it sounded like a flounder hitting marble. In that moment I think I developed a little crush on her.

She turned to me. 'Elizabeth. Greenside Memorials. Three o'clock arvo.'

'I'll be there,' I said.

'The hell he will,' said X, grimacing, and shoved her out the door.

The following afternoon, dressed as Otis on the tram north to Elizabeth, I sat next to an old drunk. I was trying to peruse the sports section of the *Adelaide Advertiser*, but he kept distracting me, reading over my shoulder.

'What do you care about our footie?' he asked, presciently. He must have gathered I was American from my confederate bandana.

'I don't. But I'm always fascinated by how nations distract themselves from their own ills through clear athletic achievement. There's twenty-two pages of this stuff.'

'Wake me when you get to the racing results,' he said and nodded off.

Later, when he awoke, I could smell him staring at me. I offered him the paper, but he waved it off.

'Those tattoos on your arm . . .' he said.

'What about them?'

'Stick-ons.'

'Yes, they are.'

'Also, that growth on your chin – utterly fake. What are you playing at?'

'I'm on my way to a funeral,' I said. 'Of some guy I don't know.' It didn't remotely serve as an explanation, but he seemed to accept it.

We rode the rest of the way in silence, and I stared out the window at the northern suburbs. Beige low-rent brick, pokies, bottle shops, junked cars withering under the austral sun – not soon-to-be a major postcard or a Baz Luhrmann film setting. Finally, the drunk spoke.

'Looking down on the unfortunate ... ridiculing bad taste and so on ... is a shallow man's version of irony. Would you not agree?'

'You're probably right there.'

'So why do it?'

'I need a perspective I couldn't have if I was being, well, *myself*.'

'Who's "myself"?'

'Rich Hall.'

'What sort of perspective might you be aiming for?'

'The third-person one. One devoid of grief or fatalism.'

'For purposes of ...'

'I dunno. Revelations, maybe. Accidental or otherwise.'

'Well, I don't buy that for a minute. And let me remark that when a bloke goes to such extremes to avoid feeling, he's nothing but a coward.'

'What would you do in my place?'

'I'd go for the shits and giggles.'

'That cancels your own advice,' I said.

'Indeed. But I'm a coward.'

We passed the waste-disposal site that X had described as hell.

'Elizabeth,' the drunk announced.

Greenside Memorial Home wasn't hard to find: a well-kept, wooden house with a lacy veranda stuck between a Thai restaurant and a TAFE vocational school. I entered the anteroom and signed the visitors register as Otis Lee Crenshaw, effectively neutralizing – I liked to think – all sentiment. Death was now palatable simply because I was make-believe.

In the main chapel, I opened the door to the thunder of thirty or so mourners, every one of them in the throes of dire rum madness. Bundy empties were strewn about the floor. Slim Whitman's yodeling curdled through some speakers. A cluster of women were gathered in one corner, consoling among themselves as if a team, while men in their best Aussie working-class formals – R.M. Williams flannel and Blundstone boots – sauntered between fixed pews, swilling, cursing, roistering in booming voices, all the while pretending this was anything but what it was: a memorial for the departed. Of course, there is death, but what can you do? Lift up thine eyes. Get trashed. Rum kills all grief.

The casket sat on a trestle at the top of the room, and I joined the small queue filing by. Edgar, elegantly reupholstered, lay with his pale hands across his sternum like a pair of delicate swallows, clutching a can of Bundaberg Rum & Cola. Also, someone had propped an Adelaide Crows pillow under his head to tilt it upward. He looked, for all the world, like he'd fallen asleep watching the footie. I laughed then reminded myself, *I have no attitude toward this*, and turned away.

From across the room, Temple appeared. She was dressed head-to-toe in stone-washed denim, including her boots, which I didn't know was possible. She swept over, plucking a can of Bundy from the table that held the floral centerpiece.

'I knew you'd make it,' she beamed. 'We're all a few of these ahead of you.'

She grabbed my hand and shaped it to the can.

I'd never tasted Bundy. It slid down my throat like plasticine. The fumes did a one-eighty and came back up as exhaust. Almost immediately I felt the gunk in my brain start to fizzle, like a self-cleaning oven. Temple saw it in my eyes.

'Chemical daydream,' she said. 'Keeps the undesirables sedated.'

She raised a thoroughly sarcastic salute to the funeral director leaning against a wall, across the room, with his hands on his hips. Beside him, a young female assistant, graduate-aged, labored to project solemnity. They both looked livid. Theirs was a solid franchise, and this roomful of drunken sluggards did not reflect the kind of mourners in the sales brochure.

'They think we don't know they despise us?' Temple said. 'Carn, mate, sticks out like a dog's bollocks.' She took a languorous swig, and I stole an opportunity to study her. I didn't quite know what to make of this girl. Her articulacy did not fit her mouth – bared, as it was, in contempt. She struck me as strong for all the wrong reasons. I realized I was weirdly attracted to her (Otis, of course, not the happily married Rich Hall), and that made for a tenuous moral jurisdiction. This 'immersion' business was a little dangerous.

'X says you're playing at this Otis Lee Crenshaw thing,' she said, abruptly. 'That it's all an act. That true?'

That staggered me and the cloud of impropriety immediately vanished. I had to take another drink to consider my response.

'I'm here as the comedian your grandfather wanted to meet,' I answered. 'And to pay my respects.'

'Fair enough. Come meet my mum.' She spun me by the back

of my shirt and led me over to a hard-looking woman standing alongside X.

'Look who's here,' X seethed, making inscrutable slits of his eyes. But he was no longer menacing, just an overgrown child hiding behind his momma.

'Mum, this is Otis Lee Crenshaw,' Temple said. 'He's the guy who writes the funny songs.'

'What songs?' You could see Mum's face was kippered from nicotine and grief.

'The bloke from TV. The one Granddad liked.'

Something in her eyes flickered. 'My god, it is. Are you going to sing for us?'

I was a bit stunned. 'I reckon that might be distasteful, ma'am.'

'What would be distasteful,' said Temple, 'is whatever dirge these numpties have programmed to shuffle Granddad off with. It would be a hoot if you sang a song, Otis. Just what he would have wanted.'

I mentally rifled my back catalogue of songs, none of which were particularly appropriate for a funeral.

'I'll write something,' I said. 'Specifically for the occasion. And condolences, ma'am. I'm sure Edgar was a nice fella.'

X crushed an empty in his hand.

'For what it's worth, *Otis*,' he said, letting my name soar with ridicule, 'Edgar was a drunk and a pill addict. With a hiatal hernia from puking too much—'

'Dry up, X,' said Temple.

'—too addled to tell the difference between R and D on an automatic shift. Put that in your song.'

I had no refutation, but it didn't matter. The rum was lifting me right off the ground and now I had a reason for being here: to eulogize someone's passing, to service the afterlife. All I needed was some inspiration. And a piano.

And more rum.

The funeral home wasn't New York City's Brill Building, but it would do. Down one hallway, I discovered a side chapel with a baby grand Baldwin in one corner. It smelled vaguely like nutmeg. I cranked the bench up to full height, necked about half a can of Bundy, then slid the fallboard back.

What to write? How do you make death funny? A good old knees-up to the departed! A shuffle. Something definably Irish. Poor Edgar, we hardly knew ye.

And it was true. What did I know of this man? Was he kind, loving, the righteous paterfamilias? Not likely. He was probably a sour wretch, done in by either his own hand or some boneheaded, automotive miscue. Not that it made a difference in this hellhole of a town, where the general view was tragic. Where, long ago, the trick to look askance was learned. To cast a neurasthenic glaze over the boredom and malaise, the filth and noise. Crack open another Bundy and let the elixir of forgetfulness slide through the space in your mouth where life knocked your teeth out. (It's possible the Bundy was making me a little morbid.)

I hammered my heels on the floor, trying to get a feeling for something bouncy, then plucked a decidedly downbeat E minor on the keys, a mortal chord. No, a shuffle wouldn't do at all. Better to start minor then resolve to major. Plangent to upbeat. A radical dynamic shift.

What I was thinking, what I was thinking – I took another slug of Bundy – *what I was thinking was . . . what was I thinking?*

Nothing. Slippage.

Never mind the melody, I decided. What I needed was words. *Words* first, then the melody would come.

I took another long pull of Bundy and stared blankly at the ivories.

Concentrate. What would Willie Nelson do? The answer was: *not be in this situation to begin with.* Generally, I thrived on these gun-to-the-head, something-wonderful-right-away moments. But the Bundy was taking me through a comet binge of shifting emotions and I couldn't seem to pin down any single particular sentiment.

I will sing to Temple. A lament for her grandfather. Like Nick Cave singing to Paula Yates at Michael Hutchence's funeral. 'Into my arms'.

I played a D, G and C.

I don't believe in an interventionist God.

Greatest opening line ever. But not mine. Fuck me, I was hammered.

Five minutes later – or maybe half an hour – I pushed myself up from the piano, scuttled over to the corner of the chapel and collapsed to the floor, curling my knees to my chin like a nautilus. I noted I was no longer wearing shoes, though I couldn't remember taking them off.

Light from a stained glass window overhead bathed the piano in an otherworldly radiance, the great wing of its lid a mast bending to the breeze on a luminous Pacific, the body a stifling hull crammed with convicts, varlets, lapsed Catholics, every one of them anaesthetized by demon rum, bumbo, grog, kill devil, Nelson's blood. Rum, rum, rum. Fiscal component of the Middle Passage, triangular trade routes, slavery, piracy, destitution, rebellion. Rum, rum, rum. Captain William Bligh, freshly deposed from the HMS *Bounty*, then self-appointed Governor of New South Wales, cowering beneath his Government House bed in mortal fright while his daughter fends off a coup d'état with an umbrella. He'd made the glorious mistake of making the stuff contraband. (Apparently, one of the attenuating qualities of Bundy was spasms of historical lucidity.)

Something came to me.

> *They used to think*
> *They made the drink*
> *That would turn the whole world upside down*

Pen, paper. I needed pen, paper. I wandered out into the hallway, Bundy fused to hand. The walls were cast in a violet gloom. I stopped in front of a mirror to take blurry stock of the person who wasn't really me: black t-shirt under a black cowboy shirt, both sleeveless, 'Brenda' – the name of all of Otis's wives – stenciled on my arm in green ink.

You're not Otis, I thought, *and you are not immersed. You're Rich Hall and you are expanded by a corrosive beverage. Capture that. Just pour it all out. A word cascade – a logorrheic slurry. And make it rhyme.*

I ended up back in the anteroom with its terrifically detailed sparseness. In one corner, another piano, a pale blue spinet.

My god, this house is full of pianos. How can you not *write songs in this house?*

I ripped an empty page out of the visitors register, snatched the pen off its chain and scribbled:

They took one sip. (E minor)
They took one sip. (B flat)
And someone said . . .

Back in the main chapel, the pastor materialized. Someone had knocked a claddagh floral arrangement to the floor. He picked it up and gingerly replaced it on its tripod, straining for patience. He counted the house and waited for everyone to take a seat, which they did not.

Eventually, he looked toward the director, who just shrugged, *Get on with it.* Slim Whitman's aural anguish faded, then disappeared. Someone kicked a can across the floor. The pastor opened his missal, looked at a page and abruptly closed it again, giving the impression he was going to wing this straight from the heart. Everyone saw this for the bullshit it was.

'Edgar Heath,' he croaked, tenting his hands, 'was a kind and exceptional man.'

'In what way?' called Temple.

'Sorry?'

'In what way was he kind and exceptional? Did you know him?'

'No, not really . . .'

'Then what the fuck are you even on about?'

Temple's mother turned to gaze at her daughter in horror.

'You're just pulling words out of thin air,' Temple continued. 'My grandfather was funny as hell, and he laughed like a drain. He loved Billy Connolly and Kevin Bloody Wilson. He loved this fella right here.' She pointed to me. 'And now he's fucking dead. So you can wipe that tragedy mask off your mug because it wouldn't fucking pass muster at the local playhouse.'

The pastor tucked his missal under his arm, bowed his head and shot out of the room.

'Tough crowd,' I said as he passed me.

Temple was now wildly energized by her own outburst. 'If anybody has any honest, decent words to say about Edgar, now's the time!'

A couple of people looked like they wanted to say something, but couldn't quite come up with anything. Temple looked over at me.

'I don't mind singing a song,' I said and braided my way to the piano at the back of the chapel. I had lyrics in my pocket, a tune pulsing in my head and a roomful of people waiting to be exalted.

The piano was a full-sized Steinway, a real ocean liner. Someone had piled boxes of Krispy Kremes on top. I lifted the lid and sent the doughnuts cascading to the floor, effectively killing the last few tremors of civility in the room.

'I didn't know Edgar,' I said, easing myself onto the stool. 'But I think he would have appreciated this.'

I took a good bracing shot of Bundy, hit an E minor and played a slow, melodious intro.

'*They thought they'd be*
The kingdom by the sea
The jewel in Australia's crown
They used to think
They made the drink
That would turn the whole world upside down
One sip and the whole world would come
For one sip . . . of Bundaberg Rum'

The congregation brayed as one. Of course. Bundy. What else in this room tied the past, present and future together, the living to the departed? Bundy!

'*They refined the sugar into molasses*
They raised their glasses high above their head
They took one sip
They took one sip
And someone said . . .'

'Yeah, hello, Department of the Interior Dialogue?'
'*Speaking.*'
'My name's Rich – I'm sorry, *Otis* – I'm performing a comedy song at a funeral in a small South Australian town—'
'*Comedy at a funeral.*'
'Yeah.'
'*Have you been drinking, sir?*'
'Profusely. And I'm about to launch into a logorrheic slurry.'

'A what?'

'A word cascade. Think *Subterranean Homesick Blues* or *It's the End of the World as We Know It*.'

'You asking for permission? Sounds like you've already made up your mind.'

'I have. I'm just wondering about textural variations.'

'Right. Keep the tempo steady. Vocally, you want to go for semi-ironic hysteria. Somewhere between Ben Folds and Weird Al. Remember to pace your breathing, or you'll pass out from hyperventilation.'

'Okay. Thanks.'

'Anytime. Good luck.'

I sang:

'Holy shit, this is liquid crack!
What the fuck are you looking at!
Come over here and I will beat you like a drum
I'll introduce your face to my hand
We'll settle this whole thing man to man
Bartender, one more can of Bundaberg Rum
'Cause its canned hate, it's liquid venom
It's semen from a demon, with just a twist of lemon
Makes you angry to your boots
Makes you wanna drive a ute
Makes you wanna take the cops on a high-speed pursuit
It's caustic soda, mixed with cola
Makes your eyes go beady, makes you go bipolar

Makes you crazy and aloof, 'til they peel you from the roof
Makes you wanna call the bouncer a big fat poof
It'll make you pissed, make you make lists
'Til you're talk, talk, talk, talk, talkin' with your fists
'Til you say something tasteless, totally racist
With no point of view or informative basis
There's something in the fermentation
Makes a man go crazy, makes him join One Nation
Makes him out of his mind, makes him hate mankind
'Til he's deaf, dumb and blind
On Bundaberg Rum.'

That sort of thing.

The mourners were rapturous. They taxi-whistled and fist-pumped the air in defiance. I caught sight of Temple's face, slack in reverie, eyes closed, lips askew. That was enough to set me on a kind of dream state in which the details of the room, the immediacy of the moment and the cornucopia of alcohol roiling in my stomach created a strange narcosis. I knew, right then, that Otis Lee Crenshaw was as dead as 'ol Edgar himself. From now on, I would write songs as Rich Hall.

I felt Temple take a seat beside me, the shape of her firm body crushing into mine.

'You know something,' she said, 'that was perfect.' Then she took my hand in hers with pure, utter simplicity and beamed a great big smile.

My last thought before falling off the piano stool was how the small gaps in her upper molars mirrored the sharps on the keyboard.

I taught the song to the band and two nights later we performed it live on ABC Television at the Melbourne International Comedy Festival Gala. It created a hell of a clamor. The cognoscenti saw it as an indictment of a certain antipodean subclass. The subclass saw it as an anthem. Every town we played guaranteed a rowdy assortment of hoons, bogans, bevans, booners and ockers. (Australia has roughly twenty-five specific variations of 'redneck'.) Proudly obnoxious, they chattered in a strangulated rural castrato, like air escaping a pinched balloon. *Strewth mate! You nailed that song. Crikey.* Lingo you could set an old watch by.

At the Sydney Opera House (The Studio, not Concert Hall – don't be ridiculous), a fistfight broke out at the bar at the back of the venue. The staff had neglected to stock Bundy – an inventory oversight which somehow culminated in a shirtless brawl between bar staff and certain belligerent members of the public, leaving chrome chairs upended and puddles of flannel adorning the floor. Imagine a Jimmy Buffet concert without margaritas.

Afterward, as we were breaking down the gear, Rob Childs, my guitarist, said, 'I have played some dumps in my life, places with chicken wire on the stage to protect us from the crowd. Sometimes the chicken wire was patched up with duct tape where people had brought their own wire-cutters and tried to get through—'

'Now you're exaggerating,' I said.

'But this place,' he said, indicating the Sydney Opera House, crown architectural jewel of the Southern Hemisphere and one of the world's most distinctive performance venues, 'is a shithole.'

We finished the tour and returned to London. In September, we recorded a live DVD at the Hammersmith Apollo. It was an absolutely stellar show. Our drummer performed from the bed of a 1952 Ford pick-up truck. We did two encores and finished with 'Bundaberg Rum'.

That was Otis Lee Crenshaw's last appearance. I packed away the piano and put him out to pasture like a spent pack-mule. When the DVD came out, 'Bundaberg Rum' had been excised. Too much of an acquired bad taste, I suppose.

INTERLUDE 3

MIRACLE AT KNOCK

And so it came to pass, on a glorious Sunday in June of 2014, a great celebration to herald the fruits of summer was held near the Holy Shrine of Knock in County Mayo, Ireland. The gathering was called the Westport Music Festival and did feature the likes of Bryan Adams, Kool & the Gang, and myself – a combination that may strike the unwashed as curious, until we consider the teachings of Christ: 'A wise man builds his house on rock, but an ensemble builds theirs on funk' (Matthew 7:24).

Here – within view of the village church, where, in 1879, appeared the apparition of the Blessed Virgin Mary – the multitudes gathered beneath a generous blue sky and there was joyous feasting. Not of oxen or fatted calves, mind, but of pulled pork sandwiches and generous lashings of coleslaw. Pre-show music wafted backstage. I was due to go on early in the afternoon and complained not a whit. 'Never take the place of honor,' Jesus said, 'but rather the lower billing' (Luke 14:7).

There sprang up a calamity. Somehow, I lost my saddle: the thin bone wedge that sits within the bridge of the guitar, which raises the strings so that the instrument can make a joyful noise, and without which makes that of a lawn rake scraping a sewer grating. It must have popped out when I was changing the strings. I fell to my knees, pawing through trampled grass, cigarette butts, chewing gum, sputum and detritus. But, alas, my search rendered fruitless. Such were the consequences that I was now too despaired to take the stage.

Behold, who should espy my plight but Tony Joe White, a song-writer who allows all to receive his truths with great pleasure – namely 'Polk Salad Annie', a staple of Elvis's shows, and 'Rainy Night in Georgia', made famous by Brook Benton – and a guitarist with some nasty, and I mean *nasty*, chops.

'Looks like you're in a bind, son,' he said, in that thick Southern drawl that sounds like molasses being strained through silk.

And indeed I was. For my appearance had been billed as 'musical comedy', and I was now bereft of the 'musical' part. Thus, I was induced to proceed empty-handed up onto the stage as there was a great and restless clamoring among the throngs for my presence.

Alas.

Before me lay a steep incline of steel ramp used for the trans-port of amps, flight cases and equipment. As there was no sedan to transport me, I had to ascend this ramp by foot. But it was slick, and the soles of my cowboy boots were leather. So traction disavowed me and, for every step forward, I slid back two in abject defeat. I floundered and reeled, grasping at the rails for the flim-siest support. My petitions for help fell on deaf ears until, at last, a roadie, casually observing my predicament, called out, 'Take off your boots, ya feckin' eejit.'

That roadie revealed himself a prophet, for – *Miracles be!* – when I removed my boots, I observed the erstwhile saddle stuck to the bottom of one sole and thus was able to summon for my guitar.

I surmounted the ramp in a state of divinity, tempered ever-so-slightly by the excruciating pain of my stockinged feet digging into rivets and raised corrugation. In that moment, I felt as one with the legions of barefoot penitents scaling the Croagh Patrick, less than a half-mile away and fully visible in the clear, exalted sunshine.

I reached the pinnacle, returned my boots to my shorn feet, slipped the saddle into its rightful place on the guitar, slung it across my shoulder, strode out onstage and, verily I tell you, *nailed* it.

CHAPTER 8

ASHLEY NO-SHOW

My dad served in the US Army as a military policeman. He was stationed at the Rhineland-Pfalz garrison in Baumholder, Germany. This was during the Korean conflict in the early fifties when America was fighting a de facto war with communism.

As a kid, I once asked if he had seen any action. He told me he had pulled his pistol on the singer Vic Damone. Vic was a fairly popular crooner back then, more or less a Sinatra lightweight. He'd arrived in Baumholder to entertain the troops and raise morale. After the show, he and his entourage – 'Goons,' my dad called them – descended on the officers' club and 'kicked up a little dust'. They were ordered to leave and, when Vic's burly bodyguard rose from the table and lumbered toward my dad combatively, my dad pulled his Colt M1911 service pistol and fired a warning shot into the club's ceiling. Compliance was quickly restored.

I heard my dad string this story out numerous times, usually to newfound drinking acquaintances at the local tavern. With every iteration, that bullet changed trajectory. It went into a nearby wall. Then directly over the goon's head. Eventually, it 'grazed Vic's thigh'. Though I accepted these elaborations as a requisite of heightened drama, I began to wonder if the incident had happened at all.

Many years later, I was walking along Columbus Avenue by Central Park in Manhattan. It was Thanksgiving morning and I'd gone up there to see the staging proceedings for the Macy's parade. Vic strolled past me, eating a cannolo. It took a moment for me to register that it was actually him. I wheeled and chased him down.

'Excuse me, Mr Damone?'

He stopped and turned. (I might have come off a bit too abruptly.)

'My name is Rich Hall. I'm a comedian. My dad claims he pulled his service pistol on you in Baumholder, Germany, in the fifties—'

'I don't have time for this shit,' Vic said. He flattened his lips against his teeth and huffed off.

'I'll take that as a yes!' I called out.

A few minutes later, I caught sight of him ambling around the festivities at a leisurely pace. I thought, *what does he mean, he doesn't have time? He's eating a cannolo. That does not signify urgency.* If someone came up and said their dad had once taken a shot at me, I believe I'd find time for them. I didn't care for Vic Damone's irrational priorities. As if to epitomize his fatuousness, a giant Bullwinkle J. Moose balloon ascended directly beyond him. It looked like Vic's inflated ego leaving his body.

*

I keep a mental catalogue of these sorts of events. I disdain most celebrities – okay, it's jealousy – so I relish those moments when they're upstaged by the scenery. Like the time I was sent to a music festival in Pori, Finland, to interview Ringo Starr for the music channel VH1. That was surreal enough. But as I chatted on camera with Mr Starr, the northern lights appeared over his shoulder. I was so besotted that I directed the cameraman to drift away from the former Beatle to focus on something of far more cosmic substance. Mr Starr ended up being an off-camera voice during most of his own interview.

Sometimes, it's the opposite: the scenery is upstaged by the celebrity. In London in 2005, I was cast in a movie called *Red Light Runners* with Harvey Keitel and Michael Madsen. We filmed for three weeks, then Mr Keitel disappeared from the set. He never returned and the production collapsed. I chalked it up to my usual bad luck with films, and Karen and I flew to Sorrento, Italy, to chill for a few days.

At the departure lounge in Naples, waiting to return to London, we ended up in an argument over some inconsequence – brought on, no doubt, by Karen's travel nerves. She was shouting in my face so intensely that I had to look past her for focus. Who do I see over her shoulder sitting in a plastic chair? Harvey himself, wearing a floral print shirt and smoking a Partagas. Karen, registering my shock, turned. Harvey held a finger up to his lips – almost a double meaning – and said, 'Meshugenah, you never saw me,' then jumped up and lost himself in the crowd.

I don't make this stuff up.

Someday, when that black Toyota Prius of Death creeps up and runs me over, I won't desire to see my whole life pass before my eyes. I don't want an image parade of loved ones or a melancholy review of my regrettable choices and decisions in life. *I don't have time for that shit.* I want to watch my deathbed highlight reel of Incongruous Celebrity Encounters. Light entertainment. Pure fluff. With that in mind, here's a question: what do Don Johnson, Ashley Judd and I share in common?

Answer: we are all cultural contributors to the United Kingdom.

Before you say, 'Whoa, Rich, check your falutin' levels because they're running a little high,' let me assure you this designation was bestowed upon me by no less than Her Majesty Queen Elizabeth II.

In July of 2012, I was summoned to Buckingham Palace to celebrate 'Americans who have made a cultural contribution to the United Kingdom'. This arrived in the form of an embossed invitation by Royal Post. I opened it and wondered briefly if it was a scam – like those Nigerian prince things, but more elaborate.

I showed it to Karen.

'It says *commanded*. Does that mean I *have* to attend?' I had a London Advertising Softball League game scheduled for the same date in Regent's Park. Against BBDO. A pretty big deal.

'Of course you have to attend. It's the Queen.'

I really have no opinion of the royal family. I could spend better time wondering why the words *swirling*, *whirling* and *twirling* are all in the dictionary since they essentially mean the same thing. And I've never even thought about that until this very moment of writing. In other words, my give-a-shit is broken.

My indifference irked Karen. I could tell she really wanted in on this shindig. She phoned the RSVP number and inquired, somewhat indiscreetly, if it was a *plus-one* kind of deal. No dice, she was told. Rich Hall and Rich Hall *only* was invited. She asked who else would be there and was informed Don Johnson and Ashley Judd would be in attendance.

Hearing those names, my attitude shifted. We are talking about a pair of cultural heavyweights.

You will know Don Johnson. He of *Miami Vice*. Pastel suits. An aversion to socks. A handgun. His commitment to Sonny Crockett – a character saddled with the near-impossible task of belonging to both the City *and* the Night (akin to bigamy, but legal) – kept millions of Americans riveted to NBC on Friday nights during the mid-eighties. *Miami Vice*'s 'no earth-tones' design diktat dramatically changed how we watched television – at least until 1990 when the show was axed, and beige items gradually sneaked their way back into the medium.

That this vaunted player has made an immeasurable contribution to British culture is above reproach. However, for the short-of-memory, let me just list a couple of pearls of Crocketonian erudition that found their way into the lexicon of the Sceptered Isle:

Tell your story walking, pal.

Hey, Rico, check out this guy's "arm". Racketeering. Money Laundering. Heroin smuggling. Whacked a rival coke dealer in Coral Gables and dumped the body off his Sunseeker Yacht . . . a real piece of work.

There was another guy who co-starred alongside Johnson. Nobody remembers his name. That's the majesty of Don Johnson.

You may have a slightly harder time placing Ashley Judd. Probably because she floats above the avowed philistinism of most British cinema viewers who swear by turgid class dramas and stories of Thatcher-devastated villages saved from ruin by boy ballet dancers, tuba-playing colliers or steel workers turned male-strippers. Ashley doesn't truck that sort of flim-flam. Her sterling performances in *Kiss the Girls* (opposite Morgan Freeman), *Olympus Has Fallen* (also starring Morgan Freeman) and *High Crimes* (with Morgan Freeman) prove that she is an actress of stunning range and versatility as long as the film has Morgan Freeman in it. It's not her fault that so many of these vehicles have succumbed to high-octane-action poisoning and non-existent-narrative logic. Ashley more than holds her own.

When not acting, Ms Judd busies herself with a dazzling array of humanitarian endeavors. She is a vocal proponent of gender equality and inalienable rights for women and girls. She is a member of the Leadership Council of the International Center for Research on Women, as well as Equality Now, and Women for Women International. She has fought sex trafficking in Cambodia, AIDS in the Congo, child poverty in Rwanda. All this, while being the face of Estée Lauder cosmetics.

And what a face! For Ms Judd has been blessed with features I can only describe as 'hermetically beautiful'. Her mouth, nose, cheekbones – even her eyebrows – turn upward toward the heavens ever so slightly, as if God had blessed her with an eternal facelift. She exudes buoyancy and cheer and seems incapable of sadness.

Yet, in several of her films, I have watched her weep – a resounding testament to her acting skills.

She is also a University of Kentucky basketball fan. That's why our souls are entwined. I make no attempt to hide my love for my Kentucky Wildcats. I grew up watching them play and still attend several games annually at Rupp Arena in Lexington. Often Ashley is there, cheering the players on from courtside.

Once, when Kentucky was playing Notre Dame, I sat next to her. A security guard hovered nearby, sweeping the stadium with his expressionless gaze. It was his job to keep the riffraff away. I could feel the distraction of the fans around us, soaking up the atmosphere of Ashley's presence, as if the outcome of the game rested on her convictions. She and I were up and down in our seats in syncopation with every exciting play. It was the best non-conversational experience I've ever shared with a woman.

When the game ended, a clutch of fans approached her for selfies and autographs. She obliged graciously. One fan also recognized me and gushed that he was an admirer of my comedy. When Ashley clocked me as someone noteworthy, her eyes crinkled and, I like to think, in that moment she accepted me into her firmament.

We were both at the Superdome in New Orleans when Kentucky beat Kansas to win the 2012 national championship. The CBS cameras were all over her, and she got about a dozen jumbotron close-ups. They cut to me several times as well but didn't zoom in enough to distinguish me from the other 60,000 fans in attendance. But because this event had happened only a few months prior in April, you can imagine how thrilled I was at the prospect of meeting Ashley Judd at Buckingham Palace to talk some serious Kentucky championship hoops. This would be my Incongruous Celebrity Encounter to beat all encounters.

Friday evening, July 13. The royal event didn't begin until seven, so I was able to get in my softball game – a stately affair with low scores. I was all over the outfield. Afterward, I rushed home, showered and got into my best suit. I had to downplay my excitement around Karen, who clearly didn't relish the idea of my spending an evening consorting with two world-renowned women without her there to run interference. She helped me with my cufflinks and didn't think it was funny when I referred to her as my lady-in-waiting.

'I doubt if the Queen is even there,' she said. 'It'll likely be a few canapes and wham-bam-thanks-for-coming.'

'She'll be there. Everybody loves to meet celebrities.'

'Well, she won't know who *you* are. Trust me.'

'Don't care, as long as I get a nice departing gift from the royal household. Maybe a small fiefdom in Scotland or something. How do you feel about serfs and vassals? Any opinion one way or the other?'

'Give Ashley my regards,' she said viciously. 'I watched *Kiss the Girls* last night. That woman does a lot of eyebrow acting.'

My cab driver was duly astounded when he was actually waved *through* the palace security gates. I dispatched from the vehicle amid the gaze of thronged tourists who were wondering, no doubt, who this man of eminence entering their sanctum of nobility was. A royal personage of some sort walked me briskly under the archway that leads into the interior quadrangle.

The quadrangle surprised me. I'd always assumed Buckingham Palace was a monolith. In fact, like many British things – the Aero and Piers Morgan come to mind – it is hollow at the core. Just a vast expanse of red, rubbery-looking tarmac. You would think someone would have filled it with statues, fountains, a bit of terrazzo, some shrubbery . . . But it looked like a tennis court without nets.

We passed through the grand entrance (badly underlit) and up the red-carpeted stairway that leads to the state rooms. My brain computed the arithmetic of coincidence: the staircase was designed by John Nash, the Regency architect; Don Johnson's most recent television foray was a detective series called *Nash Bridges*; Ashley Judd spends a good part of her time in Nashville where her mom, Wynnona, and half-sister, Naomi, performed as the country duo The Judds. The universe seemed to have momentarily tied itself up into a tidy bow.

I figured Don was going to be hanging off of Ashley and I might need some conversational ammunition to subtly alienate him from the proceedings. Thus, I planned to ask him about *A Boy and His Dog*, an obscure film he made in 1975. He stars opposite a telepathic dog named Blood. The setting is a post-apocalyptic landscape – Topeka, Kansas, actually; not much production design required. Don spends a good part of the movie forcing his shirtless torso onto the bodies of starving women, then stealing their meagre food supply. Naturally, one of his intended victims ends up falling for his charms, and the two become an item. Unfortunately (spoiler alert!), Don Johnson's dog eats her. I figured a casual enquiry into the cultural significance of any of those aforementioned details would be enough to set ol' Don on his heels and tell his story walking. In this way, I would have Ashley's sole attention. But when I entered the Blue Drawing Room, her name badge was still sitting on the reception table.

I found my own, pinned it to my lapel and gazed around. About fifty or so Americans – primarily male – milled about, most of them looking shellshocked by the furnishings, frippery, chandeliers and flocking. It felt as if any sudden movement might break something: we were at Grandma's house. A crisply uniformed staff patrolled the edges of the gathering, carrying silver trays of hors d'oeuvres at eye level – cocktail sausages with tiny American flags poking out of them. Quite a lot of imperious-looking US military brass were present, all braids and fruit salad. I wondered briefly what *cultural* contribution they were making to this island kingdom. There were other people who might be dignitaries. Academics. Olympic athletes. And there was Don Johnson.

He was totally working the room, emanating vigor and supreme coolness. My first thought was that he was much smaller in stature than his portrait, which doesn't exist, at the National Portrait Gallery suggests. He was wearing a powder blue dinner jacket and sipping sparkling water. I shot a quick look at his ankles – yep, socks. Don had made quite the effort.

After a while I worked my way over to him and introduced myself.

'Hi Don. I'm Rich Hall. Comedian.'

He sized me up. 'I see you on *Letterman*?'

'Probably.'

'Well, good to meet you, Rich Hall. Whaddya think?' I assumed he was alluding to the meticulously subdued hilarity of the event.

'Between you and me' – I leaned in – 'tackier than Graceland.'

He deflected my joke with ambassadorial perfection. 'Really? You think Graceland is tacky?' He adopted an Elvis voice. 'Don't be cruel. You're talkin' about the King.'

'If he's the King,' I said, 'how come he's buried in his own back yard like a hamster?'

He didn't reply, just flashed a Don Johnson smile and whisked away.

That was a decent enough conversational exchange, but it only got me to Memphis. I circled the room looking for the woman whose words would transport me back to New Orleans via Lexington, Kentucky. She was nowhere to be seen. I grabbed a champagne and a few sausages and made my way back over to the reception table to check if her name badge was still unclaimed. A hostess in a plum-colored dress suit was gathering up the badges and placing them into a reticule. The reticule had a royal crest and matched her jacket.

'No Ashley Judd?' I asked.

'I'm afraid not, sir,' she said with a puckish smile. She clasped the small bag shut and held it tight to her midriff. Like I was going to snatch it and run off.

Suddenly, a sense of permutation in the room. The great doors to the drawing room were closed by unseen hands. Conversations began to taper. We were all ushered into a single file. I took my place behind an admiral. I figured this wasn't the first royalty he'd encountered, so I would follow his lead since I wasn't sure what you were supposed to do when you meet the Queen. A door swung open to the adjoining Music Room, and we began to quietly ease forward.

From seemingly nowhere, a security guy stepped in front of me. Black suit, short-cropped hair, tiny microphone attached to his lapel.

'Are you Rich Hall?'

'I am.'

'Comedian?'

'Yes.'

'Please refrain from making any attempts at humor with Her Majesty.'

'Okay.'

'In fact, probably best not to say anything at all.' He turned and walked away. I did not appreciate this admonishment. What jokes was I possibly going to make? *Hey, Liz, you look much hotter in real life than your stamps. How many times have I licked the back of your head?*

The evening was becoming intolerable. It seemed to me the whole affair had nothing to do with culture. Someone had just rounded up a bunch of Americans and dragged them here on the thinnest pretext. Maybe the Queen had the hots for Don Johnson and was using us all as wingmen. I suppose my sourness was tempered by the fact that Ashley was clearly a no-show and I wasn't going to get to talk about basketball. An official greeter of some sort stepped me into the Music Room, and I found myself face to face with both a queen who had never heard of Marquis Teague, Kentucky's stellar point guard, and Prince Philip, who was taller than I expected, though nowhere near as tall as power forward Anthony Davis, who pulled down an astonishing sixteen rebounds in that Kentucky versus Kansas showdown (final score: Kentucky 67, Kansas 59).

'Your Majesty, Rich Hall. Comedian,' said the greeter. The Queen smiled wanly and shook my hand. Prince Philip misheard this and barked 'Canadian!' in a loud voice, his face registering both surprise and consternation. In that moment of confusion, here is what I imagined happened:

An ultra-sensitive microphone hidden discreetly within the concert-sized grand piano that dominated the room picked up Prince Philip's somewhat alarming pronouncement that a Canadian had infiltrated a strictly American gathering. The Royalty and Specialist Protection Command sprang into action. All entrances and barricade gates went into automated lockdown. Armed palace guards took up positions within the building, while outside a team of crack SAS personnel expertly scaled the fourteen-foot-tall perimeter fence and secreted themselves behind concrete barriers and various parapets, rifles at the ready. Three AH-64E Apache combat helicopters were scrambled into restricted airspace and deployed their Surveillance Target Acquisition and Reconnaissance (STAR) radar system. Using thermal imaging, they zeroed in on the intruder – Rich Hall – currently only inches away from the Queen. A red laser dot appeared on the back of his head.

MI6 was alerted who, in turn, notified its counterpart in Ottawa: the Canadian Security Intelligence Service (CSIS). CSIS initiated an immediate database search for the address, personal details, travel movements, financial records and criminal background of anyone in Canada operating under the moniker Rich Hall.

The Queen's Corgis were rousted, as was Theresa May, the Home Secretary (ultimately in charge of national security), who, when told there was a serious breach at Buckingham Palace, immediately began to tender her resignation, thus altering Britain's political future.

Even though I'd been instructed to not talk, the shape of history required my response.

'*Comedian*,' I corrected Prince Philip.

'Ah-hah!' he said and laughed. 'I thought I heard *Canadian*.'

This cleared up the misunderstanding, and the operation was ordered to *stand down*. Theresa May eventually became Britain's 54th – and one of its most cherished – Prime Ministers. You're welcome, Britain.

I went back to the Drawing Room and straight to the champagne table. I was a little rattled. I had never opened my mouth to the Queen and, still, I'd somehow managed to flummox both her and the prince. A fiefdom now seemed out of the question. It felt like the entire weight of the palace was coming down on me. Knocking back the champagne, I noticed a toothpick flag lying on the carpet – a desecration. *I won't have my country treated like this*, I thought. I picked it up, put it in my coat pocket, made my way out of the building and hailed a taxi to transport me back to the person I used to be.

Several years later at Rupp Arena, when Kentucky was playing their in-state rival, Louisville, I again found myself seated beside Ms Judd. She was wearing a white T-shirt with 'Big Blue Nation' emblazoned across the chest, a blue silk scarf knotted around her neck, and generating the usual small riot in her midst. I reintroduced myself and told her we'd all missed her at Buckingham Palace in July 2012.

'Oh, I really wanted to be there,' she said, 'but I had to give a speech that night at the London School of Economics.'

'What was the speech about?'

'If I remember correctly, voluntary family planning in developing countries.' Definitely a cultural contribution. *There is a lot of shit Ashley Judd doesn't have time for.* 'Did you meet the Queen?' she asked.

'I did.'

'What was it like?'

I started to answer but some strategic action under the Kentucky basket brought the crowd to its feet. I stood up and cheered with everyone else. I thought about my dad firing that bullet in Germany – the one that kept getting closer to Vic Damone and further from the truth each time he'd spun the yarn. Eventually he turned it into one hell of a story.

We sat back down. Ashley stared at me, waiting for my account. Her eyebrows looked like a child's version of birds winging in flight.

'There was an international incident,' I lied.

'*Tell* me . . .' she said.

CHAPTER 9

YOU BETTER YOU BET

One November afternoon in 2014, I walked into our kitchen just in time to hear Karen saying goodbye to someone on the phone in that way that Brits do, making the word sound like someone falling into a chasm: *'Byeeeeee!'* The diphthong of disaster, I call it.

'That was Angie Jenkinson from Teenage Cancer Trust,' she said. 'Get a load of this. The Who are celebrating fifty years together, and they've lined up a bunch of musicians to do covers of their songs. Roger Daltrey personally asked for you.'

'Cool.'

I believe I speak for most of us when I say I can't stand teenagers – the way they look right through you and skate away on something primitive with unstable wheels. But teenagers fighting cancer, robbed of the chance to enjoy the lassitude and slack-jawed abeyance of human decency, deserve all the support they can get, and I'm always excited to be a part of it.

There. That's that platitude out of the way. What I was really thinking was, *Holy shit, Roger Daltrey wants me to cover one of his songs!*

'Shepherd's Bush Empire. Next Tuesday,' she said.

'The old Empire. Proper rock 'n' roll venue.'

'Yes, but . . . Well, it's not the Royal Albert Hall, is it?'

This is an example of my wife's penchant for deflating the rosier assignments in my career. It's an excellent thing to have someone remind you of how inconsequential your worldly pursuits are, but sometimes she's vindictive about it. It's something I've watched emerge over our fifteen years of marriage. She still has her good looks, her flair for taste-making. But she long ago came to the realization that my comedy is, for the most part, a factory job minus the smokestacks.

She snatched up a piece of paper from the kitchen counter and reeled off the line-up. 'Liam Gallagher, Rizzle Kicks, Joe Elliott, Ricky Wilson, you, Eddie Vedder.'

'Wow. Is there a backing band?'

'Minus Pete Townshend. But it says here his brother Simon is playing. Also, Geddy Lee? Zak Starkey on drums? I assume those names mean something to you.'

'Yeah, they're all fairly competent.' What an understatement.

'Anyway, Angie sent over a list of songs to choose from.'

I already knew what I wanted to sing. Karen picked up her mobile phone and tapped in a number. In a moment her voice changed to a murmur.

'Hi Angie. It's Karen Hall. Rich says he'd love to do it. He wants to do . . .' She cupped the phone. 'What do you want to do?'

I started singing in a loud, aggressive voice: *'Ever since I was a young boy, I played a silver ball . . .'*

'You heard that? Oh . . . right.' She covered the phone. 'She says that song is taken. How about "You Better You Bet"?'

'Sure, why not.'

'Fine by him, Angie. "You Better You Bet." Right . . . right . . . *byeeeeee!*' She hung up. 'She says Roger will be thrilled, everyone else is afraid to go anywhere near that song.'

I could understand that. 'You Better You Bet' is a word cascade – one slip, one missed lyric, and you're chasing your hat in the wind. But since I'd proven myself the master of the logorrheic slurry, I wasn't too worried. It's also a great call and response song, and I had a picture in my head of getting the crowd to sing along and somehow offsetting my vocal deficiencies.

The first time I met Roger Daltrey was when he'd invited me to perform at the Teenage Cancer Comedy Gala at the Royal Albert Hall. That was in late 2004. Steve Coogan, Ricky Gervais and The Rutles were on the bill. I was idling backstage with Karen, who was beside herself with wonderment, gleefully reporting on every celebrity sighting. Jeff Beck and Chrissie Hynde had come up and introduced themselves. A sprightly Neil Innes had regaled us with Python stories. I could tell Karen was going to dine out on all this for months. I was studying a photo of Frank Sinatra that was hanging on a wall when Roger came up, slapped me on the shoulder blade and shook my hand effusively.

'Thanks so much for doing this,' he said in that clipped West

London inflection that sounds like someone with a mouthful of too-hot jacket potato. I introduced him to Karen, and he clocked her accent.

'Liverpool,' she explained.

'Top town,' he replied, disinclined to ask how or where we'd met.

I'd heard he was a fly fisherman, and I'd promised myself if we ever met, I would steer the conversation in that direction, but he was already ahead of me.

'Montana, right? You're a fly fisherman.'

'Whenever I get the chance,' I said.

'You know, I built a trout pond – four, actually – down in Sussex. Spring-fed. Twenty-six acres. It's the biggest freshwater reserve in the south.'

'Stocked?'

'To the brim. Big plump browns.'

'Catch and release?'

'No. I have to keep turning them over. They get too massive.'

'What kind of hatches do you get down there?'

'Oh . . . alders, damsels, sedges, olive duns.'

'Olives. My favorite fly: pale olive duns. You won't go wrong with pale olive duns.'

That this conversation was taking place under the great fluted and glass dome of the Royal Albert Hall and not a remote fishing lodge in the middle of God knows where gave it a somewhat surreal edge. Nor did Roger talk in the lugubrious cadence of most fishing enthusiasts, who turn the most mundane anecdotes into 'The Rime of the Ancient Mariner'. He chattered in a clipped, emphatic 4/4 time. Frankly, I was having a hard time imagining him delicately casting a demure fly onto the surface of a sylvan pond. This, after all, is a guy who gaffer-tapes his microphones to keep them from flying into stadia and braining people.

'Anytime you want to come down to fish, be my guest,' he said and handed me a card. The photo on the front showed Roger cradling a behemoth trout that must have weighed ten pounds. On the back was an address for his fishery in Sussex.

'Good God. This trout has its own postal code.'

He laughed. 'Like I said, anytime. Absolutely.'

'Likewise, Roger, if you're ever in Montana, my next-door neighbor is a world-class guide. *Ghillie*, I think you call them. He'll take care of you.'

'Might just take you up on that.' He shook Karen's hand and, with an athletic dispatch, shot off to greet someone else.

This exchange thrilled me no end. I've met a few rock stars before and thoughtfully resisted the urge to blather about where I saw them perform and how fantastic it was, blah blah blah. They don't remember, and they don't care. They'll tear a bookmark from your life and use it to remove something from their teeth. But I felt like ol' Roger and I had just connected.

When I looked over at Karen, she had a kind of censorious stare I'd never seen before.

'"You won't go wrong with pale olive duns",' she said in a sing-song voice. 'You had to patronize him, didn't you?'

'What?'

'Roger Daltrey just invited you to go fishing, and you felt the need to school him with your authoritarian knowledge of trout flies.'

'What are you talking about? We were just having a nice conversation.'

'Rich, he's a rock star. Rock stars don't *need* to be nice. Rock stars don't even carry a wallet. He asks you to go fishing, you say, "Absolutely, Roger Daltrey. I would love to go fishing with you." You don't stand there and pontificate.'

'Pontificate? We were just talking fishing.'

'*You* were talking fishing. *He* was talking about something precious to him. It's obvious he's very proud of those ponds, and he wants you to see them. Instead, you have to one up him with your "come to Montana" bullshit. As if you built the state with your own hands.'

She walked off shaking her head. We'd only been married for a few months. In this moment, I think I sensed a subtle change in the scenery.

Back in our London flat, she taped the card to the fridge. I would pull a beer out, close the fridge door and stare at Roger's fat, sluggish-looking fish with ever growing resentment. I knew it was ridiculous to accuse an overweight trout of being artless, but I couldn't help it. You could see that it had snaffled up anything and everything that had floated its way.

I prefer small trout, perfectly formed trout, selective trout. Call me a snob, but I've always been partial to stream fishing: feeling the current pulse against my waders, reading the water and the insect life and enjoying the rhythms of casting and the music of a screeching reel. And then there is the joy of delicately grasping a spotted cutthroat or rainbow, feeling its small weight, watching it kick free and glide away.

*

Several years passed. New marriage and old career piloted along at a self-chosen speed – though apparently not fast enough for Karen.

'When are you going to call Roger?' she asked out of the blue, as if an afternoon outing with Roger Daltrey was the entrée to a life we'd been missing out on.

'I'm not that keen on pond fishing,' I would explain. She never heard me.

'I can see it now,' she mused. 'Two men standing on a lake bank, catching fish. In that moment, it doesn't matter that one is a world-famous rock star and the other is a comic struggling to fight off serious debt.'

'We're not in debt . . .'

'All that matters is they're fishing. They cast their *pale olive duns* and feel the warm sun on their necks. In such a moment I could say, "My husband and Roger Daltrey are equals – no more, no less." Perhaps a lifelong friendship ensues.'

When Roger invited me to perform at another Teenage Cancer gig in 2009, again at the Royal Albert Hall, Karen chose not to accompany me. I think this was some form of prosecution on her part because I know how much she loved the big-ticket events, the glitz and elbow rubbing. When I got home, she didn't even ask how the performance went. She just wanted to know if Roger had asked me to go fishing again.

'He did.'

'Did he bring up the fact you've ignored him for five years?' My wife retains chastisements like bank deposits, knowing they accrue interest over time.

'No. He just said the offer was still open.'

'Tell you what I think. I think you're too intimidated to go fishing with him.'

'Why, because he's famous? I've met tons of famous people. Someday I intend to write a book peppered liberally with all the famous people I've met and how unfazed I am about it.'

'No one will read it.'

'Ask me how the gig went.'

'Don't care.'

I adore my wife when she's a noun. But when she's a verb, it's hard fucking work.

The weekend before the Empire gig, I downloaded a backing track of 'You Better You Bet' onto my phone and walked the streets of West London, singing under my breath and looking suitably deranged to passers-by.

'I call you on the telephone my voice too rough with cigarettes . . .'

Hell of a song. That very first line absolves the singer from discordance. I'm a quick read on things like this and I had the lyrics down in no time.

On Monday, I was instructed to come to British Grove Studios in Chiswick to rehearse with the band. I got there around noon, full of swagger. The studio was a chipper-looking building that seemed to be having an argument with the tired-looking, semi-detached houses surrounding it. Angie Jenkinson, radiating accommodation, greeted me at the entrance and led me into the main studio, all burnished maple and mystifying consoles. I was introduced to The Who's musical director,

Frank Simes, a nimble-looking fellow with a strange resemblance to Geronimo. A glass isolation booth with a drum kit dominated the room. Zak Starkey sat there, wielding a pair of Zildjian sticks.

Other musicians bustled about with a kind of casual-looking vigor. I immediately recognized Geddy Lee from Rush, Joe Elliott from Def Leppard, and Pino Palladino, one of rock's most stalwart bassists. Nothing in their demeanor claimed admiration for the years of rehearsals, tour bus miles, indistinguishable cities and interchangeable enormo-domes they'd played. They were merely world-class musicians doing their job. I tried to emanate a modest obedience, but inside I couldn't have been more chuffed, knowing every musician, every instrument, every component in this room was designed to make my voice sound incredibly . . . passable.

I stepped into the vocal suite, set the lyrics on a music stand and slipped on a pair of headphones. The band cracked into the song as if they were breezing through trigonometry. The sound mix was perfect in the headphones, and I had no trouble hearing my own vocals. I couldn't believe how good I sounded! If they were using auto-tune, I sure as hell didn't want to know.

Afterward, Frank spoke through the headphones. 'That song doesn't offer much runway for take-off, but you seem to have nailed it.'

'Should we run it again?'

'Only if you want to. I've got a lot of songs to get through.'

'I'm happy.'

'See you at the Empire tomorrow,' Frank said, and I bounded up to leave. I felt like a rock star.

*

One of my biggest regrets in life is not becoming a musician at a younger age. My old man killed it for me. When I was in my early teens we lived in Charlotte, North Carolina. I earned money selling Christmas cards door to door which meant that one day I dragged home a Magnus chord organ from Kaufman's Music Store. I'd been ogling the thing in the shop window for months.

I didn't get much past 'A Whiter Shade of Pale' by Procol Harum, which I blasted for weeks out of the window of my bedroom, adding to the general dissonance of the street and torturing our next-door neighbor, Mrs Laminack. I mastered the descending chord structure so aggressively that I became convinced the rock musician's life was for me and, thus, never again would I have to resort to actual speech or ideas. I bought a Nehru jacket and some orange corduroy flared trousers and strolled the school hallways with self-contained coolness. It was only a matter of time before someone would ask me to join their band.

Our house on Brandywine Avenue was thinly insulated and absorbed sound like a tuning fork, so there was no question my dad had heard me slavering away at the same song for weeks. He appeared in the doorway of my room one evening.

'It sounds like you've almost got that down, sport,' he said. He was sipping his usual early evening 'worry-be-gone' – really just a splash of Bushmills, but the delicacy of that concept compelled him to hold it stylishly between thumb and forefinger as if he were James Bond.

'Folks around here aren't as refined as you and me,' he said. 'They rarely listen to anything but Roger Miller or some primitive jazz.' I assumed by *folks*, he meant our slightly extended family which, in addition to my mom and dad, consisted of Aunt Anne and Uncle J.B., who lived next door on the opposite side from Mrs Laminack. Mom barely tolerated Aunt Anne because she chain-smoked and made only transparent attempts to be cordial. Uncle J.B. was an ex-Navy torpedo crewman with a real knack for boorishness. The fact they'd chosen to roost next door was a source of no small anxiety to my mom, especially when my dad and J.B. would get drunk and cycle 'King of the Road' ad nauseam on my uncle's old Marantz phono.

'I suggest we gather the crew together and you enlighten them with this piece,' my dad said. I viewed this invitation suspiciously. No doubt, he meant to use me to make a point to my mom about some disquieting family situation.

'It's just "A Whiter Shade of Pale",' I replied.

Apparently, he misunderstood this statement to mean 'it's not quite there yet'.

'Well, keep at it then. We'll show your mother just how wrong she is about you.' I had no idea what he meant by that.

The following Friday evening I dragged the chord organ into the living room. My mom, uncle and aunt gathered on our hideous Pepto-Bismol-colored couch. My dad stood guardedly in the kitchen doorway. Also present was Mrs Laminack, the direct recipient of my rhythmless assaults. I think the general consensus was that, once I'd performed the song formally, it would be out of my system and life for everyone could return to normal.

I made my entrance in the Nehru jacket and orange cords, plus a pair of Ray-Ban Olympians for maximum effect. My dad almost dropped his drink. He turned to my mom and said, 'Where does he get the money for this?'

I sat down in front of the Magnus and played the song in its entirety, mimicking the deadened visage of Procul Harum's lead singer, Gary Brooker, whom I'd studiously observed on the cover of an album. My audience absorbed the performance solemnly, except for Mrs Laminack, who plugged her ears with her fingers. When I finished, my aunt and uncle clapped mutely. My dad grabbed my mom by the arm, said, 'I need to talk to you for a minute,' and hastily exited to the kitchen, leaving an air of tension in the room.

The next day the instrument was gone.

'Where'd the organ go?' I demanded of my mom with a stridency I don't think she'd witnessed before.

'Your father returned it to Kaufman's.' She opened a cookie jar and handed me a clump of fives and tens: a refund. 'He was under the impression you were practicing Bach. "Air on a G String" to be precise. When he heard all those hysterics about *fandangos* and *vestal virgins*, he said, "Why is he singing, there's no singing in Bach!" Well, he's deeply disturbed.'

My dad never brought the subject up, and I guess I was too scared to confront him. We were unfathomable to each other. He read newspapers. I only read the backs of album covers. It was 1968. The nation had taken to the streets, and he was disgusted by what he saw on the evening news. Somehow, he'd decided that me cannibalizing Bach was complicit with what was going on in Chicago and Detroit.

I stuffed the outlandish costume in the back of my closet and used the refunded money to buy a white Shakespeare Wonderod and a

South Bend spinning reel. My dad and I'd fish the streams of the Great Smoky Mountains: the Mitchell, the Watauga, the Nantahala. Here the problems of the Republic – Nixon, Vietnam, yippies and hippies – couldn't interfere. All the advice he gave me on the river, he probably should have applied to himself.

'This is the only thing in life that's certain, son,' he would say, casting a slow arcing loop that seemed to hang in mid-air then parachute down onto the water. 'Trout are nature's compass needles. The current always points them true.'

'How can you be certain we're going to catch anything?' I asked.

'You're missing the point.'

I didn't touch a musical instrument again for twenty-seven years.

Tuesday afternoon. Shepherd's Bush. If you were to search carefully, a few vestiges of *Quadrophenia* still exist in the neighborhood, but it feels like the film's closing credits: the half-circle sign that leads to Shepherd's Bush Market, the faded lettering – 'Pie, Mash, Liquor & Eels' – above A. Cooke's pie shop on Goldhawk Road, now boarded up and abutted by fabric shops catering to Muslim seamstresses. Try your best to cast a nostalgic glow over this place, but it's moved on. 'Put out the fire and don't look past your shoulder,' somebody once said. At one corner of a sprawling unkempt green, blighted by a playground designed by someone who clearly hates children, looms the Empire, brute and windowless like a haunted fortress.

Inside the creaky artists' entrance, I informed the security woman I was there for the sound-check. She grimly issued me a laminate and motioned with her chin to a door that led backstage. The auditorium, swathed in darkness with the occasional island of muted light – a bar, dim exits, a sound desk twinkling like a constellation – was as mysterious and musty as an old woman's purse. The euphoria and imbecilic confidence I had experienced during the previous day's rehearsal was ebbing away. In this place something sinister felt like it was bearing down on me.

The band members skulked about the stage, shuffling through charts. I waved at them, and they grinned back wolfishly. I noticed, somewhat disturbingly, how much they now resembled their instruments. Pino Palladino with his long profile and thick veiny arms seemed to have transformed into his own bass guitar. Zak Starkey looked for all the world like a giant drumstick. Simon Townshend – or perhaps it was his guitar, for they were entwined – plucked a portentous note that hovered like the prelude to a Wild West massacre. I stepped out to the apron of the stage. The edge dropped off into black wilderness. I eased the trusty Shure SM58 mike from the stand and stood motionless.

Things quickly unraveled. The warm confines of a vocal suite like the one at British Grove, with all its appurtenances, is not, I discovered, the same as a stage with Marshall stacks, monitors and 1200-watt amps. Zak counted the song in, which begins with a chorus-like backing refrain.

'*Ooh, you better, you better, you bet . . . ooooooh . . .*'

Man, this is loud, I thought. But when the full instrumentation kicked in, it was pure detonation – a sonic shock wave that smacked me in the back of the head and caused my teeth to rattle. It came from *everywhere*. From the stacks at the sides of the stage. From the amps behind me. And from the wall of monitors standing like a line of black squalls on a horizon of aural death at my feet. I didn't even know when to start singing because the noise had pretty much blown a hole in time. And, when I finally opened my mouth, the only thing that came out was a spume of indecipherable mush:

'I fall you on the temmepho ma rose tariff woof ziggurats . . .'

I was no longer purpose, just gelatin. I grimly realized I was too concussed to remember any further lyrics, so I waved my arms at the band. The song broke down and I said, 'Can we start again?'

They started again, just as deafening. I fished the lyrics from my back pocket and more or less recited them atonally in time with the onslaught, but you wouldn't call it singing. It was about as musical as a NASA voice announcing, 'We have lift-off,' while a 300-tonne booster rocket explodes off the pad.

Afterward, Simon Townshend came over and assured me it wouldn't be so loud once bodies were in the room. At least I *think* that's what he said. His words sounded like a pair of busted woofers in the back of an old Chevy, and I wondered if I had permanent ear damage.

For a while I stood out in the empty auditorium and watched other singers sound-checking. Amy McDonald ran through a languorous version of 'Behind Blue Eyes'. It wasn't nearly as loud as what I'd just endured. Then Liam Gallagher ambulated out, dressed for permanent rain in a yellow cagoule. He snarled through 'My Generation' without ever taking his hands out of his pockets, like he was ordering something from a takeout window. More musicians followed. They all seemed to be singing at a fairly human volume, and I began to get a strange suspicion that I was somehow being set up.

I found Frank Simes and asked him if maybe the band wasn't just a touch too loud during my song.

'That's just how they play it.' He smiled. 'It's a real bone-shaker.'

'Yes, but I don't think I can do the song justice at that volume. I'm not even sure I'll get the lyrics right.'

'Doesn't matter to these guys,' he said and indicated the band. 'They're like surgeons. Big dumb surgeons. They're only concerned with the physiology of the thing.' I think I detected some sarcasm in his voice. 'If anyone actually paid attention to the lyrics of a Who song,' he surmised, 'the whole thing would collapse in illogicality. What you need is an IEM.'

'I don't have one.'

An IEM, or In-Ear Monitor, is a custom-molded earpiece musicians use to hear a clean mix while they're singing. They cost thousands of dollars. I've sung with my own low-rent band for years and never needed one. Now, apparently, I did.

'Let me see what I can round up before tonight. In the meantime, here's the advice I'd give anyone in your circumstance: go home, stand in your shower and run the lyrics until you're confident you've nailed it.'

'Okay.'

'Then turn the cold water on full blast and try it again. See how you get on with that.'

'Naked or clothed?'

'That's entirely up to you.'

'Thanks, Frank. That sounds like solid advice.' I turned to leave when something crossed my mind. 'Out of curiosity,' I asked, 'who's singing "Pinball Wizard"?'

He shook his head. 'No one that I'm aware of.'

I left the Empire and walked across Shepherd's Bush Green to clear my head. The realization that I was the destabilizing factor in an evening of wonderful music was pretty disconcerting. There was no question I was going to be flailing on that stage in front of thousands of hardcore Who fans. Would it be entertaining? Probably. In the way that watching a guy step on a rake is entertaining.

I got home and told Karen that I wasn't sure, but I had this creeping suspicion Roger was setting me up. 'Why am I the only comedian on the bill?' I said. 'Solely for Roger's amusement?'

'You shouldn't have blanked him,' she said. 'Shoulda gone fishing.'

'Again? You've been harping about that for fifteen years.'

'You think being a comedian allows you to be aloof. You've chosen to live a life of postponement. Now your chickens have come home to roost.'

She was wrong. I'm not aloof. It's just that I've always kept the social climbing stuff at arm's length because, frankly, I'm a loner. My wife has this old school idea of show business as a kind of Friars Club fraternity, that chumminess and knowing the 'right people' drives the engine of success. Me, I prefer the isolation of writing. The mechanics of performing. The *physiology* of the thing, as Frank Simes would say.

When Karen and I were first married, her eyes had been widened to a whole world of possibilities – if airport gateways and theater marquees were any indication. She must have thought we were going to be swinging from moonbeams.

I recall a wintry night several years ago at a karaoke bar in Montana. Fortified by innumerable G&Ts, she clambered up onstage and belted out Gladys Knight's 'Midnight Train to Georgia' in a tone dripping with sarcasm. When she got to the backup line 'superstar, but he didn't get far', she waggled a finger directly at me. The message was unmistakable.

Driving home in our truck, I said, 'If you see me as a failure, just say so. No need to hide it behind some Pips lyrics.'

'I don't know what you're talking about.'

'Admit it. You expected more of me.'

'I don't expect more of you. I just expect you could make more of yourself.'

'How so?'

'You're a great comedian, honey. But you're not a star. Nor do you seem to have any desire to be.'

'You should have hooked up with an astronomer. Listen, I love what I do, it's that simple. I wouldn't change it for anything.'

'Nor would I ask you to . . .'

'And I think, sometimes, when people are in love with what they do, it drives their partners a little crazy.'

'Is that so? Please explain.'

'Okay, not *crazy*. But, well, maybe *jealous* is the word I'm looking for.'

'*Jealous*? I'm *jealous* of what you do?'

'In the sense that you have to compete for the attention.'

'Oh, please. You spend all your time staring into space like an idiot. Why would I be jealous of *that*? It's pathetic.'

'As F. Scott Fitzgerald once said . . .'

'Stop the fucking truck. I'll walk home from here.'

'It's freezing outside! He said, "I could never convince my wife when I was staring out the window that I was actually working".'

'*I'm* going to stare out the window,' she announced. She rolled the truck window down and an arctic blast tore through the interior. I could no longer see. Eighteen-wheelers were barreling all around us and this particular stretch of road spat out carcasses on a regular basis.

'Any minute now, beautiful white snow is going to come floating down,' she said, sounding anaesthetized. 'I want to frolic through it. Like Robert Frost. "Miles to go before I sleep".'

'Close the window, will you?'

'Why? Can't you drive and be an asshole at the same time?'

'You're drunk.'

She wheeled around in her seat. 'Listen up, you fucking hermit. I like meeting exciting people. I like visiting exciting places. And I don't intend to die with a stash of unused frequent flyer points, get it? If we were an elderly couple, my life would be ideal. But we're not, are we? So, *impact*. Fucking well say *yes* to everything. While you've still got time.'

'That's your career advice?'

'No, it's marital advice.' She rolled up the window.

I turned on the radio, but it somehow sounded offensive. I feared another song was going to come up that she could turn against me, so I quickly switched it off again. We drove in silence for a while. The snow was coming down in fat chunks.

'Let me remind you of something,' I said.

'What?'

'I was doing this long before I met *you*.'

Shepherd's Bush Empire. Tuesday night. One hour before the show.

I popped my head out of the second-floor green room window to see a predominantly male queue stretched around the block, shuffling with decrepit animation. That's when it hit me: The Who and their fans are *old*. It was just a matter of time before the creep of dementia changed the inflection of '*Who* are you?' to 'Who are *you*?'

The green room bustled with musicians and plus-ones, emanating a kind of pre-championship game tension. I think we half-expected Roger to come bursting in and give us a pep talk on how to best interpret his own songs back to him. Ricky Wilson, the singer from Kaiser Chiefs, ambled over and introduced himself. He owns the kind of winsome good looks that instil immediate distrust, but, in fact, he was disarmingly nervous.

'I don't mind telling you, I'm shitting myself,' he said.

'Who isn't? What are you singing?'

'5.15. "Out of my brain on the train." You?'

'"You Better You Bet".'

He gave out a low ominous whistle like a movie wind that blows away footprints. What had Angie said to my wife? 'No one wants to go anywhere near that song.'

'I wanted to sing "Pinball Wizard", but apparently it's taken.'

'Not that I know of,' Ricky replied.

Karen flounced up to us, full of inchoate enthusiasm. She was wearing a floral skirt with a smart, uneven hemline and a black, menacing-looking leather jacket.

'I'm Karen Hall. You're Ricky Wilson,' she said.

'I am,' he agreed.

'Very pleased to meet you.' She raised a thin flute of Prosecco aloft as if to gauge it from a distance, downed it in one gulp and answered a question no one had asked. 'I was just talking to Liam Gallagher. I don't know what everyone's on about. He's actually, genuinely nice.' With that pronouncement, she breezed off to work another part of the room.

I loved seeing her in this kind of mood. Not twenty-four hours earlier she had interrupted my writing to inform me there was a one-eyed Boston Terrier down the street from us named Lucky Pierre who not only had his own Twitter account but had more followers than me. The best way to placate her dim view of my career, I supposed, was to occasionally rub her nose in it.

Slowly, the green room crowd began to diminish, and I figured the show must be starting downstairs. I looked around for Karen, but she was nowhere to be found. I grabbed a Heineken from the drinks cabinet, downed it, pulled the lyrics from my back pocket for a quick run-through and decided it really didn't matter what words I sang. The song was a hurricane, and you can't rope the wind. *Just gotta ride it out*, I told myself, *ride it out*.

Downstairs, the auditorium was packed. The Who fans may be old, but they aren't short on *esprit*. They jostled and swayed, calling out lustily to like-minded brethren – a carpet of jowled faces, shaved heads and bullseye-logo T-shirts sweeping to the edge of the stage. I suspected that they had been fooled repeatedly in their lives, that they had uniformly failed to die before they got old and now they were here for one more jump-start, like a scrapyard of broken-down cars awaiting one last glorious ride. Something subtle in the lighting changed – it was hard to tell if it was a fading or a brightening – but the crowd sensed it as one and a great roar rose forth. They began to stamp their feet and shout, and I stood off in the stage wing feeling gusts of fear rolling over inside me. An offstage voice announced, 'Ladies and gentlemen, please welcome your host for the evening . . . Chris Evans!'

Out came the bespectacled radio guy, looking like an owl trapped in a centrifuge. He muttered away, more or less talking to himself, about how we were all there for teenage cancer survivors. The crowd absorbed this blandishment like they were watching an infomercial. You could tell they wanted this fellow swiftly out of the picture and, when the band emerged and took their places, the roar started up again.

I felt a tap on my shoulder and turned to see a stout fellow in a grey auto mechanic's shirt whom I mistook for a techie. His sleeves were rolled up ridiculously high as if he was prepared for some strenuous lifting. But all he held in his palm was a small orb.

'Rich Hall? Eddie Vedder.'

'*Oh.* Hi. Good to meet you, Eddie.'

He handed me the object. 'Frank Simes said you needed an IEM. Use this one. I always carry a spare.'

'Thanks. How's it work?'

'It takes a little getting used to.' He started to demonstrate, but the music suddenly kicked off from the stage. (As irony would have it, it was 'Can't Explain'.) I stood there and watched Eddie's lips moving and nodded along like a dullard. He mimed a kind of complicated gesture that indicated, I believed, that I was to insert it in my right ear and secure it with tape. God knows if that was what he meant at all. He shot his thumbs up to signify good luck and disappeared into the dark.

I went on fourth on the bill, right after the hip-hop duo Rizzle Kicks delivered an almost unrecognizable but inspired version of 'The Kids Are Alright', turning the crowd's initial bafflement into ultimate, utter delight. It was the proverbial hard act to follow. Nor did it help that Chris Evans, with champion ineptitude, introduced me as 'Rich Wilson'. I walked out to a somewhat perplexed reaction.

The song started up as soon as I hit the stage, the backing vocals signaling its arrival from a mile away: '*Ooh . . . you better, you better, you bet . . . ooh . . .*'. The crowd bellowed its recognition, and the room compressed into a great sucking vacuum of expectation. I had the IEM lodged in my right ear, held in place by a thin strip of gaffer tape. I opened my mouth to sing.

'*I call you on the telephone my voice too rough from cigarettes . . .*'

The sound in my left ear was a deafening canyon of noise. The sound in my right ear was my own voice, pure and crystalline, calling down to me from atop a high, high mountain. It was like I was in two places at once, and I immediately understood what Eddie had meant when he said 'it takes a little getting used to'. The goddamned thing gave me vertigo. I began to feel dizzy and weightless.

The panic in my head intermingled with the lyrics coming out my mouth and I sang something to the effect of *'I got your body right now on my mind but . . . I CAN'T JUDGE MY DISTANCE!'* which I believe is not in the original version of the song.

I was no longer sure of my footing. The room tilted on an invisible fulcrum. To get my bearings, I used the microphone as a sextant, lining it up against the balcony at the back of the theater. I put a foot forward and felt nothing but air, realized I was at the very edge of the stage and stepped back, stumbled over a monitor and lurched so violently that the IEM – tape intact – flew out of my ear and into the crowd where it momentarily attached itself to the lapel of a full-length leather coat worn by a burly fellow with declining but still distinct mod aspirations. The mod guy reached his hand up to brush it away, and I watched in horror as the IEM detached itself from the tape and sank like a prawn to the lightless bottom of an ocean floor.

I dropped to my knees and began gesticulating wildly in the general direction of where it had fallen, a gesture that ran counter to the lyrics I was singing at the time:

'I don't really mind how much you love me. Oooh, a little is alright . . .'

No one in the crowd had the slightest inkling what I was trying so urgently to convey. They simply stared in bewilderment at a man singing one song while acting out an entirely different one. I leaned further out over the crowd. This was roundly misinterpreted as a desire to crowd surf and several bodies shoved me back. A man raised his palms like a traffic cop and shouted, 'I've got a gammy leg!' Another one warned, 'I'm not insured, mate,' and threatened to douse me with a plastic cup of beer. The mod guy reached up and casually affixed the strip of gaffer tape sans the IEM to the top of my shoe. Asshole.

Eventually, the song reached a protracted instrumental part. As the band chugged away muscularly, I used the interlude to pronate myself, crawl forward and drop the upper half of my torso over the edge of the stage, scanning the floor for the elusive little bastard. Thus, the audience was now treated to the sight of what appeared to be a man vomiting violently over the side of an unsteady boat. I was aware of the pop of flashbulbs, the hovering of mobile phones, the eternity of YouTube hell.

Then I spotted it. Glistening up from the floor. A woman with silvery-red hair piled high atop her head and great owlish glasses saw what I was pointing to. She bent down, retrieved it and began to examine it curiously. I wiggled my fingers impatiently and said, 'C'mon lady, don't act like you've never seen a hearing device before.' This was picked up in the mike and broadcast loudly around the room, ultimately to be credited as *additional baffling lyrics by Rich Hall.

The woman deposited the IEM into my outstretched hand. I jumped to my feet with a mixture of triumph and relief, and instinctively looked toward the stage wing. I saw Eddie Vedder bouncing up and down jubilantly. I saw my wife, horrified, her palms against her face like the Home Alone kid. I saw Liam Gallagher openly laughing (that might have been an historic first). Then, just before I launched back into the vocals, I caught sight of ol' Roger himself, seated at the very end of the first row, next to Angie Jenkinson. They were both doubled over with hysterics.

I closed out the song with the rousing call and response I'd planned all along:

Me: 'When I say I love you, you say . . .' Crowd: 'You better, you better, you bet!'

I like to think, in the crowd's estimation, this salvaged the performance. I can't say for sure. But when the song finished there was thunderous applause. Or, possibly, a roar of catcalls. I couldn't really tell because all I could hear inside my pulverized eardrums was a sound like a loud rope slapping against a flagpole.

I've been to a few rodeos in my life and seen bull riders tossed about like rag dolls. Invariably, they crawl to their feet, pick up their hat and use it to sweep the sawdust and dirt from their boots. I've always been curious why. If you've just been kicked, gored, crippled and humiliated, what's a little sawdust on your boots?

That night, as I stood in front of 3,000 Who fans, inelegantly peeling a strip of gaffer tape from the top of my shoe, I suddenly realized why: it's the only dignity you have left.

That following summer Karen and I went fishing on the Yellowstone in Montana. My old neighbor, Mark Bolton (the ghillie) took us out in his ClackaCraft drift boat. He rowed us to a quiet turn in the river and we sat there and waited for the hatch. Mark has rapid eyes and a darting nature that looks for everything, and right now he was following the silky currents of the stream. Nothing was rising yet – it was still too cold – but we knew it was only a matter of patience. He'd once said to me, 'Nature is a department store and trout fishing is the Lost and Found.'

It was Karen's first time. She sat with the fly-rod planted in one hand like a grenadier. In the distance, the mountains rose like the beginning of a Paramount movie. It was breathtaking.

'Can you imagine Roger Daltrey and you fishing this river together?' she said.

I could. I now wanted more than anything to bring Roger here. He would appreciate that these mountains were nature's Marshall Stacks, the river – illuminated by the sunlight breaking over the cottonwoods – a glorious stage. He would be as overwhelmed by the sheer magnitude of Montana as I had been overwhelmed that night at the Empire. And with any luck, he would fall overboard, and I could watch *him* flail for his life.

'Let me ask you something,' I said to Karen. 'That day that Angie called, and I said I wanted to sing "Pinball Wizard" . . .'

'Yeah?'

'Did she really say it was already taken?'

She didn't answer right away. Mark, who had been quietly listening in, sensed the void and pointed out, apropos of nothing, that he was never much of a Who fan and personally preferred Mott the Hoople.

'Of course she didn't,' Karen finally said. 'But why would you do anything *that* predictable?'

Later, on her very first cast, Karen caught a small rainbow. *Jesus, the luck of that woman*, I thought. I reached over the side and netted it. She cupped it in her hands, and it throbbed, vital as any heartbeat, while I unhooked the fly. Then she loosened her grip on it, stood up in admiration and we watched it spiral away.

CHAPTER 10

ESSENTIAL

I once tried to insure my sense of humor. I was making a show for the BBC called *Badly Funded Think Tank*, and the director Chris Cottam and I flew to Orlando, Florida, where there are more insurance brokers per capita than any city in the world. The premise was: if Bruce Springsteen could insure his voice, and Betty Grable could insure her legs, then I should be able to insure *my* most valuable asset.

Chris filmed me as I went from agency to agency, trying to get a policy. Naturally, we got laughed out of most places. But Cliff Eidson of the Eidson '(We Insure Anything') Insurance Agency, Edgewater Drive, Orlando, proved amenable.

'It's doable,' he said, from behind the desk in his office, located in a strip mall between a laundromat and a nail salon. 'But how do I know you're funny?'

I'd brought along a garden rake. I stood up, laid it on the floor and stepped on it vigorously. The handle shot up and caught me right on the temple. Cliff practically fell out of his chair. We both wiped the tears from our eyes. But Chris missed the shot and I had to do a second take. This time, the rake handle whacked me above my left eye. A huge, red welt was already forming over the right one.

'Are you covered for personal injury?' Cliff asked. 'Because that looks serious.'

He said he could insure my sense of humor, but it would be very expensive. Probably around 20,000 dollars. So I declined.

Years later – 2020, to be exact – Covid dropped the floor out from under my world. My tour was canceled midway through. That would be the last time for quite a while that I was *allowed* to do what I do: stand on a stage and make strangers laugh. This is not said to elicit sympathy. I accept that I am not essential. But it sure as hell blindsided me.

I probably should have bought that policy.

My touring show was called *Hoedown*. The first half was straight stand-up – the usual wry invective about the world and all its problems. The second half was musical, an attempt to take the country music ethos and apply it to Britain. There were a lot of crafted songs, but also improvised tunes based on talking to audience members. 'What do you do?', 'Where are you from?', 'How did you two meet?' kind of stuff. I much preferred that half. It was looser and more improvisational.

Early in the tour, I'd played the Oxford Playhouse. You get a really varied crowd in Oxford: academics, scholars, luminaries, forklift drivers, plumbers. The show was sold out. But there was one guy in the very front row with an empty seat beside him. He was older looking, carelessly attired and observing me with heavy, Germanic attention. He never once laughed. There are few things more infuriating onstage than an ice-faced audience member. Finally, I stopped in the middle of a routine and said, 'What's with the empty seat, fella?'

He looked a little startled.

'I'm envisioning the possible scenarios,' I said. 'And none of them are particularly encouraging. You have a wife or a partner. You said, "I have two tickets to see Rich Hall." Your partner said "No." So that's a tandem rejection we share. It's bad for me because it reminds me there are people out there who don't think I'm funny. But it's worse for you because you and your partner obviously share a sense of humor, or you wouldn't be together. Yet, your lone presence makes me think I drove a wedge into that relationship. I'm the homewrecker.'

Laughs, but of the nervous kind. I think the audience felt like I was picking on the guy.

'Where are you from?' I asked him.

He took a moment to answer. 'France.'

'Ah! What do you do?'

'What do you mean?'

'For a living.'

'Why do you ask?'

'Well, in case you haven't noticed, I have a guitar and three musicians behind me who are waiting for this vital nugget of information so we can improvise a song around it.'

His shoulders stiffened, and he seemed to be pushing his weight into his chair. 'I don't want to say what I do.'

'Okay then. I guess this is going to be an instrumental.'

That got a good laugh, but I felt stung. Humorless people have no business coming to a comedy show.

Later, when I was in the middle of a song, the Frenchman rose from his seat and headed up the aisle for the exit. Another figure – a hulking fellow in a sharp grey suit – appeared from the side of the room and trailed close behind him. The crowd witnessed this, and it made for a palpable distraction. From this second man's steely gait, I sensed he was assigned security.

After the show, while the band was loading up, I went up to the front of house to thank the theater staff. The lobby bar was still open and the Frenchman was there, sitting at a table with the bodyguard. The bodyguard had a big ruddy, friendly face. He saw me and shot a thumbs up. The Frenchman leaned over, said something, to him, then stood up and came toward me.

'Can I buy you a drink?' he said.

'No,' I answered. 'You walked out on my show.'

'Why did you ask me what I do?'

'Look, I didn't mean to make you uncomfortable, okay? I guess you're some kind of big deal or something.'

He didn't acknowledge that. Instead, he said, 'I saw you some years ago in Paris, at the Hotel Du Nord. My colleagues and I shared a table at the back. You sang a song called "Let's Get Together and Kill George Bush". You made a lot of jokes about America. We were very loud and obnoxious, but we thought you were very good. Tonight . . .'

'What about tonight . . .?'

'I was offended. You weren't rude enough.'

'Sorry?'

'The first half of your show was . . . irresponsible and excellent. You made jokes about Trump and Syria and racism. You talked about corruption and hypocrisy. It seemed essential.'

'There's nothing essential about stand-up comedy. It's just expedient.'

'But, the second half, you just came out and played music.'

'And . . .?'

'You are, I think, both prolific and lazy. What do you gain from singing songs to people in the audience about their occupations?'

'It's fun. It's celebratory. It's ridiculous.'

'But what point does it make?'

'It's not a point. It's a counterpoint.'

'I think, when you are angry, you are very effective. When you sing to the audience, not so much.'

'Look, I'm not getting any younger. I don't want to be the angry old guy going onstage every night and ranting for two hours. That's just sad. And ineffectual.'

'And you want to be effectual?'

'I just want to be funny. Jokes can't change the world, friend.'

'Then why be a comedian?'

'Why be anything? Because I love it. And I'm good at it.'

'I agree. It is an important gift, one not to be wasted.'

'You seem to be struggling to get something across.'

'Would you like me to tell you what I do?'

'I honestly don't give a shit.'

He reached into his jacket pocket and pulled out a felt marker. 'You say jokes can't change the world.' He grabbed a napkin from the bar and – with very deft, quick movements – made a small illustration. He handed it to me. It was a cartoon drawing of a Muslim man: elongated nose, ping-pong balls for eyes, a scraggle of beard and a drooping turban. It was comical, ridiculous and sinister at the same time, and it had taken the Frenchman all of twenty seconds to draw it.

'That little chap changed the world,' he said.

Then it hit me. Hit me like nothing had ever hit me before. *Of course* he wasn't going to say what he did for a living. Not during my show, anyway. It would have devastated the room. I know, because it devastated me, just standing there.

I studied his face. He wasn't really all that old. He just looked old.

'I think I will have that drink with you,' I said. 'Do you still draw for that magazine?'

'Yes.'

Then I asked him what I was really thinking, what I really wanted to know: 'Tell me something, do you still have a sense of humor?'

'No,' he said with his thin, heart-breaking smile. 'But I still have my balls.'

I thought about that moment a lot during the fifteen months of imposed lockdown. I wondered what it was like to be able to *create* comedy without *feeling* it. Probably, I concluded, no worse than *feeling* comedy without being able to *create* it – my situation at the time.

Like I said, this is not a plea for sympathy. I chose this profession. You become a comedian when you see the cascade of problems in the world or the human condition and, knowing you can do nothing to change it, decide to make your living ridiculing it. We pretend to share a common cause with the secret lives of everyone, but we don't. We're professional wise-asses, bullshit detectives, word engineers, swindlers. Comedians and con artists have everything in common. Outsized egos. The same patter. The same inflections, tone and pacing. Information is on a need-to-know basis only. Every word is misdirection. The only difference is, while con artists relieve one person of a large sum of money, comedians relieve many people of a small sum of money. And here's the best part: the robbed love it and come back for more. What a racket!

I despair at the homogeneity of the modern profession. The first true generation of alternative stand-up was rife with rebels, renegades and self-saboteurs: Bill Hicks and Sam Kinison come to mind – their lifestyles informed their comedy. They worked without a net and they paved the way for the next generation, who, for the most part, toned its habits down to moderate excess. I can think of very few present-day comedians whose comedy is a by-product of risky living. Doug Stanhope comes to mind. Even he knows not to take himself too seriously. If Bill Hicks were alive today, I've no doubt he would be a conspiracy freak, succumbed to the black gravity of alt-bias and the feeling of superiority that accompanies it. He would be influential and truly dangerous.

The newest generation of anomalous comics approach their craft with the diligence, passion and charisma of chartered accountants.

They mine personal catharsis for crowd communion. They've never done anything risky or dangerous with their lives, and it shows onstage. If I'm coming off bitter, it's because I've been hosed with some of the highest auto insurance rates in the world and these lightweights hardly justify the outlay.

The gigs started trickling back in the summer of 2021. In August, I was booked to play the Pine Creek Lodge in Montana, a glorious outdoor stage set against the backdrop of the towering Absarokas. A creek runs through the venue. If you don't bring your own camp chair, you sit on a log.

I knew a lot of friends, acquaintances and neighbors would show up, particularly Mark Bolton, apostate to all humor. His withering presence would be unsettling and I wanted to be sharp. Someone told me there was an open-mike night over in Bozeman. They weren't quite sure where – either the Elks Club or the Moose Club, both fraternal organizations whose initiation requires fidelity to antlers. I figured I'd go up there and run some new stuff. Also, it was an opportunity to check out the burgeoning new Montana comedic talent.

The Elks and Moose Clubs sat on opposite sides of Main Street, both with hidden off-center entrances and an ancient neon crest proclaiming 'Benevolence, Loyalty, Brotherhood', and all the other words that are code for 'cheap drinks and no loudmouths'.

I chose the Elks and went inside. Downstairs was almost empty – just a few guys cradling Budweisers, watching baseball on a muted TV. There was some crowd noise coming from upstairs, so I bought a beer and headed up.

It was just a function room, badly lit. I leaned against a back wall and counted maybe forty souls in attendance. There was no stage to speak of, just a mike stand in one corner, where a big, friendly-faced man of thirty or so worked the crowd. He wore a grey jacket that might have once been part of a suit ensemble, pressed jeans and a worn pair of cowboy boots. His great shoulders sloped, as if his buttoned, tieless collar weighed too much on his neck.

'I love single-malt whisky,' he said. 'Couldn't get enough of it. My girlfriend used to say, "If you can afford single-malt whisky, why can't you take me out to the Black Angus once in a while for a rib-eye?" I'd say, "Damn, sweetheart, you gotta shut up. This single malt is older than you. Show some respect for your elders . . ."'

I thought that was a pretty good joke, but no one laughed. That's when I realized I was at an AA meeting. I left and headed across the street to the Moose. Outside the comedy room, there was a hand-written notice warning the audience that the show contained possible 'anxiety triggers'. I asked the young comedienne who promoted the show what that meant.

She explained: 'A lot of people in the audience are emerging from isolation. We're a little worried that comics might say something that induces "re-entry stress".'

Wow. The rot is everywhere now. From worrying about offending the world's biggest religion to traumatizing a small Montana gathering, placation is paralyzing modern stand-up. I'm not saying offensiveness is essential to comedy. But when comedy becomes afraid to even *risk* offense, well we should all just take up balloon modelling.

The comedians who took to the Moose Club stage could not remotely be described as polished, confident or engaging. They were misfits: sartorially distressed, contemptuous, caught between the constrictions of their 'woke' sensibilities and the need to self-flagellate. Almost all of the punchlines were inwardly directed.

'I hit a deer with my car. I cradled it in my arms and its dying words were "I never got to do the things I wanted to do with my life".'

'My gran passed away last week. It's only now that I can laugh about it.'

The only truly offensive comedy is bad comedy. I went back to the Elks. I figured the alkies would be far more entertaining.

CHAPTER 11

RAKE

My last ever comedy gig was in a small pub on the outskirts of London. It was February 7, 2030. I cracked the room up. Big belly laughs. I knew then it was time to pack it in.

This, of course, was after public laughter had been proscribed. The No-Tickling Law, enacted in 2027 by the newly formed Department of Body Autonomy, was initially meant to protect children. But it quickly expanded to include all individuals. A year later, during the Third Puritan Awakening, it was deemed that inciting laughter was a form of verbal coercion, and to force an audience to chuckle out loud was akin to making them yell 'Fire!' in a crowded theater. (Substitute 'Snort-plee-hee-hoo-hoo' for 'Fire!') The government told us it was for our own good.

Most of us stand-ups gave up after that and drifted off into the soft-focus of distant memory. Jo Brand returned home to South London, filed for divorce and spent all her time rescuing Dalmatians. (The coastal inhabitants of Croatia, not the dogs.) Jason Manford went back to Salford. He found God and preaches now. Stewart Lee bought a scissor lift, got drunk one night on absinthe and ran the bucket into some high-tension wires – that'll be two years ago come April. John Bishop works as a stevedore on the Liverpool docks.

Jack Dee got a server's job at the seafood and champagne bar in Terminal 8 of Heathrow Airport. I ran into him on the street a few months back. He was carrying oysters in a plastic carrier bag.

He told me, 'You can't crack 'em open on a wet mattress.'

I took that to mean he was homeless.

I guess we all learned the hard way that right doesn't always mean equal, and equal doesn't always mean fair.

For those of us who hung in there, it was a real struggle. We tried to move forward, to adapt to the idea of *laughter-less* humor. The secret was to write jokes that had to be processed by the brain before they could reach the gut, thus suppressing any involuntary bronchial response, i.e. a laugh. I mostly traded in abstruse one-liners. Example: 'I ordered breakfast at a German restaurant. The waiter bought me two small dots on a plate. I said, "I'm sorry, I ordered an *omelet*."' The crowd – what was left of them – could be counted on to smile painfully but never emit a single chuckle. Yeah, I was *that* good.

Why was I still doing comedy? Because it's all I knew, and it's all I'll ever know. I couldn't get it out of my system, try as I might. I wasn't ashamed to be performing in front of twenty, maybe thirty people. A crowd is a crowd. You don't measure it by numbers . . .

Enough, Rich. Are we really taking the surreal angle now? Have you run out of real-life stories?

No! It's just that I can't fathom my future ending any more than I can fathom this book ending. I don't want to get off the page any more than I want to get off the stage. I look back at my life and it's like looking through the wrong end of a telescope directly into another telescope. The most precise details of my vast and panoramic career are magnified *and* distorted.

I recall an old man who once came up to me after a show in Bridlington in 2028 and gave me a little figurine he'd carved out of birdseye maple. The figurine was of me, detailed right down to my cowboy hat. He told me I was his fifth favorite comedian. I hugged that man, and we both sobbed openly.

Crowds have shown me how much hurt there is in this world, but also how much love. I don't even know what that means but it sounds like something a comedian should say at the end of a book. And I believed with all my heart, that when the world came to its senses, laughter would return. Until then, I just had to do what I do best. Go up onstage and perform to abject silence.

The gig that last night was in the upstairs room of the Rose & Crown in Hampton Wick. The room filled with about forty people – a discerning audience. They brought their own tambourines and, if they really appreciated a joke, they would shake them vigorously. That's how you knew when you were killing: the room sounded like a Hare Krishna gathering.

Two of my favorites were on the bill. The Irish comedian Dylan

Moran had a great routine about James Joyce's Stephen Dedalus arguing with a traffic warden over a parking ticket. Very outré, very egalitarian. Bill Bailey had perfected a masterful musical interlude imagining himself as an apprentice to Salvador Dalí, tasked with making floppy clocks. I was in esteemed company that night.

I was introduced, walked out onstage to the rattling of expectant tambourines and promptly stepped on a rake. (I'd placed it there before the show.)

I don't know how it went so wrong. I'd misjudged the crowd's collective refinement. I figured they would see a man stepping on a rake as a postmodern deconstruction of physical humor. They would see I meant to be ironic. But when that handle smacked me square in the middle of my head, they fell out of their seats. Howled. Wept with laughter. Couldn't help themselves. I let that glorious sound drench me like desert rain over a man dying of thirst. It was the sweetest thing I'd ever heard.

Within minutes, The Humor Renunciation Tactical Squad burst into the room and cleared the place. I was dragged to the Hampton Wick Police Station, interrogated, fingerprinted and threatened with deportation. It made all the papers, of course, and the platform shamers – Spapoop, Glibster, Zzzyzzyx, Flitterbook, et al. – had a field day. In the end, I got off with a £1,000 fine.

The Rose & Crown had it worse. The council ordered the place torn down. I went there to say goodbye. A light rain was falling, the air an admixture of vindication and bereavement. Some of the bystanders – real tar and feather types – were delighted to see it go. But a handful of comedians were present as well, including

Bill and Dylan. We stood together with our arms entwined, three old men – me the eldest. Our eyes distant and glazed with trance. The demolition crew, working with a delicacy that was all the more touching for their burliness, dismantled the exterior, brick by brick, timber by timber. Some of the crew were crying.

They moved us all up to a knoll for safety, and someone set off a dynamite charge. When the dust had settled, all that stood was a lone mike stand, proud and defiant, like the sapling that survives the wildfire, on a rubbled stage.

You can't kill comedy. There will always be those of us who think the unthinkable, speak the unspeakable and laugh in the face of all decorum. We're the misfits, the ones who reach out to the wet-paint bench of opprobrium and smudge it with our stubby little thumbs, then wipe it on a passing dog. (Please, please, don't ever reprint that last sentence.)

I felt a jab under my armpit. Bill was tickling me. I reached over and tickled him back. Then Bill reached over and tickled Dylan. Then Dylan reached out and tickled me. Then the three of us went at it – in full view of renegades and Puritans alike – until we collapsed in a heap of hysterical laughter and tumbled to the bottom of the hill.

ACKNOWLEDGEMENTS

Special thanks to Kris Bailey, Merrill Markoe, Marc Beaudin at Elk River Books in Montana, Marlene Zwickler in Edinburgh, and the talented Robbie Fulks for his Fountains of Wayne Hotline inspiration. And especially, especially . . . to Leith Johnson for her unstinting and invaluable assistance.